Royal Fireworks   Language Arts   by Michael Clay Thompson

POETRY
and humanity

Michael Clay Thompson
Royal Fireworks Press
Unionville, New York

Sir, I admit your general rule,
That every poet is a fool,
But you yourself may serve to show it,
That every fool is not a poet.

- Samuel Taylor Coleridge, "Epigram"

Royal Fireworks Press
First Avenue, PO Box 399
Unionville, NY 10988-0399
(845) 726-4444
FAX: (845) 726-3824
email: mail@rfwp.com
website: rfwp.com

ISBN:
Student Book: 978-0-88092-662-1

Printed and bound in the United States of America using vegetable-
based inks on acid-free recycled paper and environmentally-friendly
cover coatings by the Royal Fireworks Printing Co. of Unionville, New
York.

Table of Contents

Poetry and Humanity

Almost all art is about humanity.

Human beings are the seeking species. We seek
to understand what is outside of ourselves, and we
seek to look within ourselves.

We want to know who we are. What we are.
Why we are. We want to understand the sources
of joy, and sadness, and meaning. We want to understand
what it means to be alive.

We want to understand love. And sorrow. And courage.
And loss. We want to understand how to reach
our dreams, and how to find out what our dreams should be,
and how to bring happiness to our family and our friends.

We want to understand what it means to be good.
We want to know how to know the right thing.
We want to care about something important,
something greater than ourselves.

We want to see the humanity of all humanity,
and to understand those things that all of us, everywhere,
have in common.

Like other artists, poets have turned their attention
to human existence, pushing language to its maximum
in order to express those things about humanity
that are most true, or difficult, or subtle.

Sounds of the Voice

Different artists use different materials
to express what they see and think.
Painters use color and texture, shadow and form.
Composers use notes, rhythm, and harmony.
Sculptors use stone, metal, wood, balance, and shape.

Poets use their own good materials.
They use the materials of language. Of the voice.
They use words, but within the words,
they use sounds.

A poet might use a fluty sound, like
the *oo* sound in the word *lute*

ooooooooooooooooooooooooooooooooooooooooooooooo

Or a soothing, hummy consonant, like the murmuring *m* in *Mary*

mmmmmmmmmmmmmmmmmmmmmmmmmmmm

Or a scratchy, spiky sound, like the harsh *k* sound
in the word *bleak*.

kkkkkkkkkkkkkkkkkkkkkk

Look, for example, at how British poet
Thomas Hardy used the scratchy *k* sound, and its good friends
the hard *g*, *b*, *d*, *p*, and *t* sounds, to suggest the severity of the English winter,
and by extension a form of profound pessimism, in his 1902 poem
"The Darkling Thrush":

I leant upon a coppice gate
    When Frost was spectre-gray,
And Winter's dregs made desolate
    The weakening eye of day.
The tangled bine-stems scored the sky
    Like strings of broken lyres,
And all mankind that haunted nigh
    Had sought their household fires.

The land's sharp features seem'd to be
    The Century's corpse outleant,
His crypt the cloudy canopy,
    The wind his death-lament.
The ancient pulse of germ and birth
    Was shrunken hard and dry,
And every spirit upon earth
    Seem'd fervourless as I.

At once a voice arose among
    The bleak twigs overhead
In a full-hearted evensong
    Of joy illimited;
An aged thrush, frail, gaunt, and small,

In blast-beruffled plume,
Had chosen thus to fling his soul
Upon the growing gloom.

So little cause for carollings
Of such ecstatic sound
Was written on terrestrial things
Afar or nigh around,
That I could think there trembled through
His happy good-night air
Some blessèd Hope, whereof he knew
And I was unaware.

If we were to delete all of the other letters from the poem,
and just look at the harsh *g*, *b*, *d*, *p*, and *t* consonants, and put
a dash to indicate new lines, it would look like this:

tpcppgt—tpctg—dtdgddt—kd—
tgdbtcdkktgbk—dkdttd—dtd—dptdb—
tcptt—cptcdcp—ddt—tpdb—kddd—
dptp—d—t—bktgd—td—td—dgtd—
btbdp—dt—pgg—ttcc—cttd—tttt—d—
tcdkbd—ppgdt—bdp—d

It is a kind of Morse code, tapped out in tough consonants,
to let us know that the scene is serious—cold, sharp, and inhuman.
It is quite astonishing; Hardy has filled every crack of the poem with severity.
Poets often do this—use vowels and consonants as a kind of
sound effect, as the music behind the plot.

But wouldn't any group of, say, two hundred words
have some *k*'s or *g*'s? Well, that would be likely,
but we would not see the defining presence of such
sounds. Clearly, Hardy has poetically pushed the harsh sounds
to the front, probably tripling or quadrupling the
incidence of such sounds, and making it impossible
to read the poem in a sweet or soothing way.

That is why even though there are also some softer
consonants in the poem, they do not cancel out
the harsh sounds. The soft ones are overwhelmed
by the harsh ones, and pushed back into the shadows
of our attention. This dominance happens
in reverse, too. When a poem is predominately made
of pretty and soft vowels and consonants, its few
normally scratchy-sounding sounds take on the
tone of the overall poem, and can even sound
pretty because of their context—because of the way
they work with the sounds beside them.

In what way are soft sounds soft?

In William Shakespeare's *Romeo and Juliet*,
Shakespeare always gives Juliet beautiful sounds to speak,
like *f*'s, *th*'s, *wh*'s, *r*'s, *n*'s, *m*'s, and *o*'s. These are sounds that sing
and that blend softly with the sounds next to them.

In the famous balcony scene, where the hidden Romeo is listening
to Juliet talk about him, she reflects that it is just his name,
Montague, that is her enemy, since the two families are feuding.
Why, she complains, must you be a Montague!
Look at the soft and pleasant sounds that Shakespeare
gives her lines:

10

'Tis but thy name that is my enemy.
Thou art thyself, though not a Montague.
What's Montague? It is nor hand, nor foot,
Nor arm, nor face, nor any other part
belonging to a man. O, be some other name!

Notice that there is not one *k* sound in the passage.
And notice how the words tend to *begin* with soft sounds, that set
the tone: *thou*, *though*, *other*, *nor*, *foot*, and even *Montague*.

When a painter paints a sunset with a red and purple sky,
he or she does not paint the entire painting only in a two-tone
red and purple style. For the complete painting, there may
be dozens or even hundreds of colors and shades. Poetry is
like that. Shakespeare would not use *m*'s and *r*'s exclusively
for Juliet's language; rather, he would work through the words,
blending in touches of softness throughout the passage, in a
way that would have an effect on those who hear the words,
but not be showy. He did not want Juliet's lines to sound
like a tongue-twister. The point is not to call attention to the sounds,
but to use the sounds artistically, secretly,
to bring the character to life.

What if we wanted to capture the sound
of beautiful fabrics, the rustling and whishing
sound that cloth makes? We might use lots
of *s*'s, *th*'s, *f*'s, *sh*'s, and soft vowel sounds
such as the *ih*, *eh*, and *ah* sounds. The
poem might be like this:

Cactus and Rock

Michael Clay Thompson

She'd seen this day, distant mirage, shimmer,
Wished it were here, instant, with words that friends
Would say, to find her in these clothes, with beads
And feathers, silver rings, and things. Now this,
Her visions of admission, membership—
Her childhood ends, new role, intense,
Full member of the tribe. In moccasins,
Hair brushed long, lockets, earrings, pendants
Falling over ceremonial robes,
She knows the path ahead,
Between the cactus and the rocks,
Round the mountain
In the desert heat,
Like a mirage,
To the infinite.
A tumbleweed rolls silently
Across the path.

3

Patterns of Sound

Like stripes in a baseball shirt,
or the woven pattern of a lawn chair,
the sounds of our voices can form patterns.
A shirt might change from gray to blue, to gray to blue,
and a poem might repeat the same sounds
over and over, even though the sounds
appear in different words each time.

Poets make patterns with sounds.

RHYME

When words end in the same sound,
such as *word* and *stirred*, that is **rhyme**.
If the rhyme is one-syllable, such as
complete and *defeat*, that is called
masculine rhyme. The rhyme is two-syllable,
with the second syllable unstressed,
such as *calling* and *falling*,
that is called **feminine rhyme**.
When rhymes come at the ends of the lines
in a poem, that is called **end rhyme**,
but if a rhyming word is found inside a line
of poetry, that is called **internal rhyme**.
Good rhymes, such as *fluff* and *tough*, do
not have to be spelled alike; it is a matter of sound.
Imperfect rhymes, such as *George* and *surge*,
are called **near rhymes** or **slant rhymes**.
And words that look like rhymes but don't
sound the same, like *cough* and *rough*,
are called **eye-rhyme** or **sight rhyme**.

rhyme
rhyme scheme
alliteration
assonance
consonance
reversal

internal
near rhyme

masculine
end rhymes

XXI
Emily Dickinson

He ate and drank the precious words,
His spirit grew robust;
He knew no more that he was poor,
Nor that his frame was dust.
He danced along the dingy days,
And this bequest of wings
Was but a book. What liberty
A loosened spirit brings!

The Irish poet William Butler Yeats (pronounced *yates*)
used **near rhyme** at the beginning of his poem "Easter 1916."
Here are the first four lines; *day* and *gray* are **masculine** (one-syllable)
rhymes, but *faces* and *houses* are a sort of **feminine** (two-syllable) **near rhyme**.

> I have met them at close of day
> Coming with vivid faces
> From counter or desk among gray
> Eighteenth-century houses.

Yeats used **eye-rhyme** in his poem "Under Ben Bulben."
Ben Bulben is the name of a mountain in County Sligo,
Ireland. The second part of the poem begins with the lines:

> Many times man lives and dies
> Between his two eternities.

What do you think the eternities are?

Even though *dies* and *eternities* look the same in their
last three letters, *ies*, they do not sound the same.
Dies rhymes with *eyes*, but *eternities* rhymes with *breeze*.
Dies and *eternities* are **eye-rhymes**. Alfred, Lord Tennyson,
used **eye-rhyme** in his poem "In Memoriam A.H.H." It is
a long poem; here is a sample:

> Again at Christmas did we weave
> The holly round the Christmas hearth;
> The silent snow possessed the earth,
> And calmly fell our Christmas eve.

Percy Shelley used brilliant combinations of **masculine** and **feminine**
end rhyme in his 1820 poem "To a Skylark." Here is one stanza (part)
of the poem:

> We look before and after,
> And pine for what is not:
> Our sincerest laughter
> With some pain is fraught;
> Our sweetest songs are those that tell of saddest thought.

Shelley was adept at finding rhymes with very different spellings.
After and *rafter* would be easy to think of, but *after* and *laughter* seem
less noticeable. Interestingly, Robert Browning also
rhymed *after* and *laughter* in his 1851 poem "Memorabilia":

> But, you were living before that,
> And also you are living after;
> And the memory I started at—
> My starting moves your laughter.

And then William Butler Yeats took up the *after-laughter* rhyme again
in his 1938 poem "Under Ben Bulben":

> Sing the peasantry, and then
> Hard-riding country gentlemen,
> The holiness of monks, and after
> Porter-drinkers randy laughter.

It turns out that many poets have rhymed *after* and *laughter*.

Sometimes, poets emphasize near rhyme
over perfect rhyme. William Blake made heavy
use of **near rhyme** in his 1789 poem
"On Another's Sorrow." Here are the first
two stanzas:

Why might near rhyme be better than perfect rhyme here?

> Can I see another's woe,
> And not be in sorrow too?
> Can I see another's grief,
> And not seek for kind relief?
>
> Can I see a falling tear,
> And not feel my sorrow's share?
> Can a father see his child
> Weep, nor be with sorrow filled?

scheme

Blake used three pairs of **near rhymes**:
woe/too, *tear/share*, and *child/filled*. By doing this
he put the rhymes in the background; the poem
sounds more like ordinary talk, like real questions. Because
the subject of care, of compassion, of our ability to sympathize and
participate in the sorrows of another, are so important,
Blake wanted to make sure that the ideas, not the poetics,
were foremost in the readers' attentions.

Rhyme Scheme
Notice that in each stanza, Blake rhymed line one and two,
and then rhymed line three and four. We would say that
his **rhyme scheme** was aabb ccdd. We describe the rhyme scheme of a poem
by assigning the letter *a* to the first rhyme, the letter *b* to the second,
and so on.

Simba
Michael Clay Thompson

She left the village, down the trail,	a
Her feet so cool against the soil, the pail	a
Light now, with water from the well	b
It would be heavy, splashing. She could tell	b
The sun would soon be flashing; breeze	c
Came through the leaves. From the acacia trees	c
The yellow hornbills' easy cry, and she replied,	d
"Ooo woo! Ooo woo!" They flew. Beside	d
Her came that dog, Basenji, wagging tail	a
And ears alert for creatures in the grass.	e
They walked together now, the shady trail	a
A-buzz with insects, crickets hopped, they passed	e
The turn and then the well appeared—	f
She stopped. Fresh tracks—a simba—lion, when	f
It came she wasn't sure, but recently—she feared	g
It was there now. The grass was still. A weird	g
Look in Basenji's eye—he knew—she backed up	h
Edging toward the village, moving slow,	i
"Let's go, Basenji, now," she thought, then stop,	h
A noise, just barely, in the grass. O, no.	i
Basenji froze, his neck hair rose, a low growl	j
Came from down inside, and then a miracle!	j
Out from the tall grass stepped her father,	k
Smiling. "I'll help," he said, "get the water."	k

ADVANCED RHYMES

At first we are tempted to think that a rhyme is a rhyme,
period. What else is there to know? Well, there is a great deal,
and poets have explored almost every rhyming possibility imaginable.
A few examples:

Half-double Rhyme

In a **half-double** rhyme, the last syllable of one word
rhymes with the next-to-last syllable of another!
The words *man* and *savanna* are examples.

Elided Rhyme

In an **elided rhyme**, there are two syllables that would
be a perfect rhyme except for the vowel in the second syllable.
The words *livid* and *lived* are an elided rhyme.

Amphisbaenic Rhyme

In **amphisbaenic rhyme**, two syllables are identical,
but in reverse! Examples would be *stick* and *kits*,
kill and *lick*, or (almost) *Nile* and *lion*.

Reverse Rhyme

In an ordinary perfect rhyme, the final syllable (or more)
of two words sounds the same. What if the entire first syllable
of two words sounds the same? That would not be alliteration,
because in alliteration, only the first vowel or consonant sound
is alike. When words share the first syllable sound,
such as *na*tive, *na*ture, *na*dir, and *na*tion, that is **reverse rhyme**.

Half Rhyme or Apophany

Apophany is when two syllables share their beginning and
ending consonants, but not the vowel in between. The words
stand and *stunned* are apophany, as are *cattle* and *kettle*.

Believe it or not, this is just the beginning. Just an introduction.
There is much, much more to learn about rhyme.
Becoming a professional poet means acquiring real knowledge,
and wonderful but hard work. The finished poem, if it is well done, will seem—
but not be—spontaneous and effortless.

rhymes

ALLITERATION

We have learned many interesting
things about rhyme. Rhyme can repeat
one syllable, or two; it can come at the end
of the line, or in the middle. It can be perfect,
or just close. It can rhyme to the eye,
but not to the ear.

But what else can we do with words?
What else can we repeat in order to make patterns?

Well, if rhyme is repeating how words end,
then one alternative would be to repeat how words begin!
Just as words like *hoop* and *dupe* end alike,
words like *snail*, *statue*, *supper*, and *soap*
begin alike. They all start with the same sound.
So do *open*, *oats*, *ocean*, and *onerous*.
Peter Piper picked a peck of pickled peppers.
When words begin with the same vowel or
consonant sound, that is called **alliteration**.

fierce
fiery
fight

In William Shakespeare's play *Julius Caesar*,
Caesar's wife, Calpurnia, begs Caesar not to go to the capitol
today because of the terrible omens that are occurring,
including a great storm in the night. She describes events:

> And graves have **y**awned and **y**ielded up their dead.
> **F**ierce **f**iery warriors **f**ight upon the clouds
> In ranks and squadrons and right form of war,
> Which drizzled blood upon the Capitol.

As this passage from Shakespeare implies, alliteration is not unusual. It is one
of the most common of all poetic techniques, and it can
be extremely effective.

ASSONANCE

In alliteration we use words that repeat the same
beginning sound. The alliterated sound might be
a vowel, or it might be a consonant.
But what if we just repeat a vowel sound, even
if it is neither at the beginning, nor at the end?
What if the vowel sounds occur in the middles of the words?
Repeating a vowel sound is called **assonance**.
For example, we could repeat, and therefore emphasize,
the *oh* sound in *photo*, *mole*, *bologna*, *nose*, and *hope*.
Notice that none of those words rhyme,
and none of them are alliterated!

CONSONANCE

If we repeat a consonant sound,
that is called consonance!

RHYME:	boat, mote
Repeated **endings**	
ALLITERATION:	silly, sole, send
Repeated **beginnings**	
ASSONANCE:	roam, soap, home
Repeated **vowels**	
CONSONANCE:	open, apply, impish
Repeated **consonants**	

In other words, we can make patterns out of any sounds we like!
We can repeat the ends of words, the beginnings, or the middles.
Poets sometimes use all of these patterns in the same poem, filling
the poem with patterns of sound.

Look at the first stanza of Henry
Wadsworth Longfellow's poem "Snow-Flakes."

Out of the bosom of the Air,
Out of the cloud-folds of her garments shaken,
Over the woodlands brown and bare,
Over the harvest-fields forsaken,
Silent, and soft, and slow
Descends the snow.

What is
your favorite
line in this
poem?

Q

Alliteration: *brown, bare*
Alliteration: *Silent, soft, slow, snow*
Alliteration: *folds, fields, forsaken*
Masculine end rhyme: *slow, snow; Air, bare*
Feminine end rhyme: *shaken, forsaken*
Assonance: *Out, cloud, brown*
Assonance: *bosom, woodlands*

Or look at this passage from Algernon Charles Swinburne's
poem "An Interlude":

In the greenest growth of the Maytime,
I rode where the woods were wet,
Between the dawn and the daytime;
The spring was glad that we met.

Alliteration: *greenest, growth*
Alliteration: *woods were wet*
Alliteration: *dawn, daytime*
Masculine end rhyme: *wet, met*
Feminine end rhyme: *Maytime, daytime*
Assonance: *greenest, between, spring*
Consonance: *rode, woods, glad*

We will frequently see an adjective alliterated with its noun, as in *greenest growth*.

26

We begin to realize that poems really are poems!
They are not just lazy prose lines with rhymes at the ends,
but poems all the way through. Look at these two stanzas
from Thomas Hardy's poem, "Channel Firing," about
the British navy practicing gunnery at sea, and waking
up the skeletons!

That night your great guns, unawares,	a
Shook all our coffins as we lay ,	b
And broke the chancel window-squares,	a
We thought it was the Judgment-day	b
And sat upright. While drearisome	c
Arose the howl of wakened hounds:	d
The mouse let fall the altar-crumb,	c
The worms drew back into the mounds.	d

See the alliteration in *great guns, howl hounds, mouse mounds*; the consonance
on the k sound in *shook, coffins, broke, squares, wakened*; the assonance on the *uh*
sound in *guns, unawares, Judgment, crumb, drearisome,* and *upright*? There is powerful
consonance on the *ow* sound of *howl, hounds, mouse, mounds*. Just look at all of the
variations on the *o* sound: *shook, coffins, broke, howl, arose, hounds,
mouse, worms, our, thought, window*; the poem howls. The whole poem
is a roaring sound track for the plot, which is about roaring guns.

ook

crum

un hou

coff

uns mou how

alliteration (g)

consonance (k)

assonance (uh)

internal rhyme

That night your great guns, unawares,　　　a
Shook all our coffins as we lay,　　　b
And broke the chancel window-squares,　　　a
We thought it was the Judgment-day　　　b

end rhyme

assonance (ou)

And sat upright. While drearisome　　　c
Arose the howl of wakened hounds:　　　d
The mouse let fall the altar-crumb,　　　c
The worms drew back into the mounds.　　　d

assonance (oh)

alliteration (h)

assonance (ah)

alliteration (m)

assonance (ow)

There is more. In order to capture the feeling of navy artillery roaring in the English Channel, Hardy has combined all of these *ow*, *oh*, *uh*, *ou o*-based vowel sounds with a series of special consonants, called **stops**. These consonants all have in common the fact that they stop the air flow through the mouth, just for a split second, causing a little burst of air to follow, like a small explosion.

The **stopped consonants** are *P* and *B*, *T* and *D*, *K* and *G*. Each pair makes its stop in a different part of the mouth. Say them aloud, and you will feel the change happening in your mouth. If we simply ask, did Hardy use consonant stops in "Channel Firing," we discover:

That night your great guns, unawares,   a
Shook all our coffins as we lay,   b
And broke the chancel window-squares,   a
We thought it was the Judgment-day   b

And sat upright. While drearisome   c
Arose the howl of wakened hounds: d
The mouse let fall the altar-crumb,   c
The worms drew back into the mounds.   d

William Butler Yeats wrote a softer, but equally
powerful poem about the joyful innocence of the young,
who have not yet encountered life's hardest days.
The title of the poem is "To a Child Dancing in the Wind."
Can you see alliteration? Do you find the eye-rhyme?
Do you see the internal rhymes in lines one and six?
Do you see assonance connecting lines ten and eleven?
What vowels and consonants does Yeats include, to capture
the feeling of the scene?

What does
Yeats mean
by "the fool's
triumph"?

Dance there upon the shore;	a
What need have you to care	b
For wind or water's roar?	a
And tumble out your hair	b
That the salt drops have wet;	c
Being young you have not known	d
The fool's triumph, nor yet	c
Love lost as soon as won,	d
Nor the best labourer dead	e
And all the sheaves to bind.	f
What need have you to dread	e
The monstrous crying of wind!	f

Of course, this can go too far.
If a poem becomes too burdened by technique,
like an over-decorated Christmas tree, the result is not art.
Some poets, such as Emerson, felt that Edgar Allan Poe
was guilty of tedious excess in technique; in fact, Emerson called
Poe "the jingle man" because of the obvious, even overpowering,
sound patterns in Poe's poems.

Some poets have written spoofs of poetry, to show
what bad poetry is like! One of the funniest poems ever written was
by the brilliant Edward Lear, who wrote "Cold Are the Crabs"
to ridicule technical overkill, to parody weak-minded sentimentalism,
and to mock foolish self-seriousness. Read dramatically, if you dare:

Cold are the crabs that crawl on yonder hills,
Colder the cucumbers that grow beneath,
And colder still the brazen chops that wreathe
The tedious gloom of philosophic pills!
For when the tardy film of nectar fills
The ample bowls of demons and of men,
There lurks the feeble mouse, the homely hen,
And there the porcupine with all her quills.
Yet much remains—to weave a solemn strain
That lingering sadly—slowly dies away,
Daily departing with departing day.
A pea-green gamut on a distant plain
When wily walruses in congress meet—
Such such is life—

Which do
you think is
the funniest
line?

How funny! Look very carefully until you think you have found
most of the techniques. The poem is loaded with alliteration. There are
internal rhymes. And if anyone can tell us what this poem means,
he or she must be a genius!

A RHYME LAB

It would be fun to experiment with all of these patterns of sound. Let's write a poem, as an experiment, trying (1) to fit in as many of these different patterns as possible, and (2) to make a statement about the value of all humanity. Elements could include end rhyme, masculine rhyme, feminine rhyme, eye-rhyme, internal rhyme, half rhyme, alliteration, assonance, consonance, elided rhyme, amphisbaenic rhyme, near rhyme, and half-double rhyme. The result could be something like this:

Flying Fish
Michael Clay Thompson

The rusty freighter rolled, great green swells rose,
Elbows on the crusty rail she thought about
The scenes she'd seen, thought close, as she began
Her voyage home. Those children laughing in Angola, she
Remembered them, their voices—after that the mother in Sudan
Who grabbed her boys up when the soldiers came, she ran—
The old man in Calcutta making chess men, carving on
The cold tile floor, eyes light and clear with calculation,
His smile bright as she replied, her salutation—
Fancy dancers eating limes along the miles of Amazon—
Farmers in the pampas, Argentina, vast horizon,
Cracking campfires smoking with the smell of sizzling steaks—
That temple in Japan, the soft and silent faces
Of the worshippers, devotion deep, meant, not temporary, traces of an
Inner peace, a place—That rushing boatman on the Yangtse River pushing
Off the dock, his wife and children waving at her, flattered,
On the deck—All those children calling from the train
In Mississippi, voices falling, waning, as they raced away, way
Down the clattered track, the painted boxcar claiming (boasting):
Southern Serves the South.
The harbor mouth lay far behind, faint coastline.
A lone flying fish broke from a swell,
And sailed, small ghost, lost across the foam.

4

METER

METER

When we talk about rhyme and its variations, we are
at least talking about patterns that we can not only hear
but in most cases see. Alliteration is usually evident to the eye,
and words that rhyme usually look alike.

But there is a fundamental part of poetry that cannot
be seen; it can only be heard, and it often takes some practice
to learn to hear it. It is called **meter**, the pattern of stressed and
unstressed syllables that poets arrange in order to control
not only the vowel and consonant sounds but also the rhythm
of the sentence, the rise and fall of the **stresses**.

Imagine a sound-effects machine that creates a wave sound;
an approaching wave would sound louder, stronger, and then
the sound would fade until the next wave came, and then the
wave sound would grow louder again.

Why
is meter
not
seen?

Our voices are like that. Without even thinking about it,
we give more volume and emphasis to some syllables, and not
to others. This emphasis is called **stress**. For example,
we say CHICKen, not chiKEN; baNAna, not BAnana or banaNA.
The word *fruity* sounds like FROOtee, not frooTEE.
The name Bobby is pronounced BOBee, not boBEE.
We pronounce *misery* MIZZeree, not like *Missouri*.

It is the same in Spanish. Each syllable is either stressed or unstressed.
The word for friend, *amigo*, is pronounced ahMEEgo, not ahmeeGO.
When we learn the vocabulary of a different language, we have to learn how to stress
the words, just as we do when we learn new words in English.

How do you say *calamity*? Don't you say kaLAMMitee?
The second syllable is stressed. What about *refrigerator*?
We say reeFRIJerater. Not refriJERater.
Leopard is LEPPerd. *Mushy* is MUSHee, not muSHEE.
Forlorn is forLORN, and *goofy* is GOOfee.

What if someone came up to you and said,

It SEE bit SEE spy DURR.

Would you understand? Probably not. But if they said,

IT see BIT see SPY durr.

You would know at once that you were hearing a nursery rhyme.

Itsy bitsy spider.

Look at these two stanzas from a poem by Emily Dickinson.
We'll put stressed syllables in purple. What do you notice?

The moon is distant from the sea,
And yet with amber hands
She leads him, docile as a boy,
Along appointed sands.

He never misses a degree;
Obedient to her eye,
He comes just so far toward the town,
Just so far goes away.

A pause like this in the middle of a line of poetry is called a **caesura**.

Yes. Every second syllable is stressed. Dickinson has carefully
arranged all of the words in the poem so that the rise and fall of
stresses is perfect, an exact rhythm. The question now becomes, what is
the **pattern**? What is the pattern of stresses that repeats in the poem?
In this poem, the pattern is a two-syllable group, with the first syllable
unstressed and the second syllable stressed. Then that pattern repeats itself,
all the way through the poem.

The **moon**　/　is **dis**　/　tant **from**　/　the **sea**

In *Alice and Wonderland*, Lewis Carroll wrote
a poem about the Walrus and the Carpenter at the beach:
The fourth stanza is:

> The Walrus and the Carpenter
> Were walking close at hand:
> They wept like anything to see
> Such quantities of sand:
> "If this were only cleared away,"
> They said, "It would be grand."

The pattern of stresses is just the same as we saw in Emily Dickinson's
poem:

Each line has four of these two-syllable patterns, and we would call each one
a **foot**. In other words, each line has four **feet**, four two-syllable **feet**.

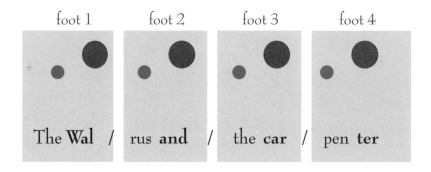

38

Once we understand that a **foot** is a stress pattern that is repeated in a poem, and that this foot-based rhythm is called **meter**, we begin to wonder, "What are the possibilities?" Wouldn't it be possible to make lots of different rhythms in poems? Couldn't we create beats in poems, similar to drum beats? Yes. Just as we saw that poets have deep understandings of the intricate possibilities of rhyme, we will see that they also have deep understandings of the possibilities of meter.

Even though, in truth, there are shades of stress, with some stressed syllables being even more stressed than others, we think of syllables as either/or: they are either stressed or not. This means that we create our stress patterns with a sharp sense of clarity, like the dots and dashes of Morse Code.

What does this imply?

Well, it means for example that there is no one-syllable foot. A line of poetry in which every syllable were stressed, or unstressed, would have no repeating pattern. It is the combination of stresses and unstresses that makes the pattern.

The next possibility is that a foot would have two syllables, as we have seen. Yet all of the examples we have seen were of two-syllable feet with the second syllable stressed. Can the first syllable be stressed instead?

And is there such a thing as a three-syllable foot?

Let's look at the four most common types of foot in traditional poetry. On the following page, we'll have an overview, and then we can explore in detail afterwards.

The Two-Syllable Foot

IAMB, iambic
An iamb is a two-syllable foot with the stress on the second syllable.
The iamb is the most common foot in English poetry. It has a natural sound.
Examples: *below, maliciousness, a never-ending night, Mine eyes have seen the glory of...*

TROCHEE, trochaic
A trochee is a two-syllable foot with the stress on the first. It is also common.
The trochee is an anti-iamb; it often has an evil feel.
Examples: *mustard, happy, chicken fingers, lurking menace, double trouble*.

SPONDEE, spondaic
An anapest is a two-syllable foot with both syllables stressed.
Spondees are often used for emphasis in a line of iambs. They are not unusual,
but unlike iambs and trochees, there are no poems made entirely of spondees.
Example (italicized): And suddenly ahead there was a *huge wave*.

The PYRRHIC FOOT
An anapest is a two-syllable foot with both syllables unstressed. Poems are not
written entirely in the pyrrhic foot; it is used for rhythmic variation, to break up
the too-regular sound that may occur with perfect iambs or trochees.
Example (italicized): And sudd*enly* ahead we saw the wave. Appar*ently* it worked.

The **Three-**Syllable Foot

DACTYL, dactylic
A dactyl is a three-syllable foot with the stress on the first syllable.
Many poems are written in dactyls.
Examples: Hand him the, happily, whether the. Onward and onward and onward...

ANAPEST, anapestic
An anapest is a three-syllable foot with the stress on the third.
Examples: On the top, analytical tree. If an elephant's trunk was as long...
T'was the night before Christmas when all through the house...

AMPHIBRACH (AM fih brack) (RARE; listed for scholarly interest)
An amphibrach is a three syllable foot, with the middle syllable stressed.
The adjective *fantastic* is a natural amphibrach. The Greek
stem *brachy* means short, and *amphi* means both. An amphibrach is a foot
that is short at both ends! *aMOEba, gaLOSHes, exPLOsion*

AMPHIMACER (am FIH mah sir) (RARE; listed for scholarly interest)
An amphimacer is also a three-syllable foot, but in this case the middle syllable is short,
and the first and third are long! *ANoDYNE, ULtraLIGHT, MACerATE*

English poems are traditionally written in iambs, trochees, dactyls, or anapests,
though many modern poets use loose cadence rather than regular meter.

As you read on the previous page, there are four main types
of poetic foot in English poetry: iambs, trochees, dactyls, and anapests.
Iambs and trochees have two syllables, dactyls and anapests three.
By far the most common of these four is the iamb. Why?
Because the English language is naturally iambic, and so poems
in iambic meter sound real and reassuring to us. Often, iambic meter sounds
benevolent, or reflective. Here is a poem, "Crossing the Bar," by Alfred,
Lord Tennyson; it is written almost entirely in iambic meter.
It is about the hope of eternal life, comparing entering the afterlife to crossing
the final sand bar and entering the deep sea.   Tennyson wrote it
when he was eighty years old.

Sunset and evening star,
And one clear call for me!
And may there be no moaning of the bar,
When I put out to sea.

But such a tide as moving seems asleep,
Too full for sound and foam,
When that which drew from out the boundless deep
Turns again home.

Twilight and evening bell,
And after that the dark!
And may there be no sadness of farewell
When I embark;

Where is
the narrator
embarking
to?

For though from out our bourne of Time and Place
The flood may bear me far,
I hope to see my Pilot face to face
When I have crossed the bar.

Alfred, Lord Tennyson
1809-1892

Let's look closely at some of the lines and inspect the iambs.
Some of the lines have **five** iambs (iambic pentameter):

          1   2   3   4   5
And may / there be / no moan/ ing of / the bar,

          1   2   3   4   5
But such / a tide / as mov / ing seems / a sleep,

          1   2   3   4   5
When that / which drew / from out / the bound / less deep

          1   2   3   4   5
And may / there be / no sad / ness of / fare well

          1   2   3   4   5
For though / from out / our bourne / of Time / and Place

          1   2   3   4   5
I hope / to see / my Pi / lot face / to face

These lines are placed between others that have **three** iambs (iambic trimeter):

          1   2   3
When I / put out / to sea.

          1   2   3
Too full / for sound / and foam,

          1   2   3
And af / ter that / the dark!

          1   2   3
The flood / may bear / me far,

          1   2   3
When I / have crossed / the bar.

What effect does he get by changing meters?

44

Finally, there are a few odd lines, in which the iambics are
different or slightly displaced. The line "When I embark" is a two-iamb line.
Most interestingly, the second line, "And one clear call for me," has a **spondee**!
The words *clear* and *call* would both be pronounced with emphasis,
and Tennyson gave them even more emphasis by alliterating them. See:

1   2   3

And one / **clear call** / for me!

The clear call is the summons from eternity; having come from eternity,
the "boundless deep," there is now a clear call to go back to eternity
and "turn again home." And it is good; there should be no grief, no
"moaning of the bar," no "sadness of farewell." A *bourne*, by the way,
is a stream; life has been a bourne of Time and Place, and now it is time
to embark back, cross the bar, and meet the Pilot face to face.

The iambic meter of the poem creates a smooth environment of dignity
for the words. The rhythm is not bumpy. The poem feels peaceful and untroubled. The
alliterated *f*'s (*full, foam, from, face, flood, farewell, far*) create
a soft background soundtrack for the ebbing tide.

1   2   3   4   5

But such / a tide / as mov / ing seems / a sleep,

1   2   3

Too full / for sound / and foam,

Looking further at the poem, we see that Tennyson divided the poem into groups of four lines; we would say that these are four-line **stanzas**, which are called **quatrains**. We will discuss stanzas at great length later. We also notice that the poem used end rhyme, and that he rhymed the first and third, and second and fourth lines. The rhyme scheme of the poem is abab, cdcd, efef, gaga; in other words, in the fourth stanza, Tennyson went back to the very first rhyme sound of the poem, and rhymed *bar* with *star*. This return of the rhyme reflects the return of the soul to its home in the boundless deep; like the soul, the rhyme returns.

Which stanza is your favorite? Why?

Sunset and evening star,
And one clear call for me!
And may there be no moaning of the bar,
When I put out to sea.

But such a tide as moving seems asleep,
Too full for sound and foam,
When that which drew from out the boundless deep
Turns again home.

Twilight and evening bell,
And after that the dark!
And may there be no sadness of farewell
When I embark;

For though from out our bourne of Time and Place
The flood may bear me far,
I hope to see my Pilot face to face
When I have crossed the bar.

Notice also that although most of Tennyson's lines have punctuation at the ends, creating pauses, some of the lines do not pause. Look at the last two lines in the second stanza, the last two lines in the third stanza, and the first and third lines in the fourth stanza. In these lines we would read right through the rhyme, rather than pausing on it. A line that pauses or stops on an end rhyme is called **end-stopped**, and a line that reads through the end rhyme is called **enjambed**. Tennyson used a combination of end-stopped and enjambed lines. What difference does this make? Well, look at the fourth stanza; by enjambing the first line, Tennyson developed a straight run of eight iambs, sixteen syllables, without a pause; the line says that the "flood may bear me far," and the long enjambed passage goes far.

Sunset and evening star,	end-stopped
And one clear call for me!	end-stopped
And may there be no moaning of the bar,	end-stopped
When I put out to sea.	end-stopped
But such a tide as moving seems asleep,	end-stopped
Too full for sound and foam,	end-stopped
When that which drew from out the boundless deep	**enjambed**
Turns again home.	end-stopped
Twilight and evening bell,	end-stopped
And after that the dark!	end-stopped
And may there be no sadness of farewell	**enjambed**
When I embark;	end-stopped
For though from out our bourne of Time and Place	**enjambed**
The flood may bear me far,	end-stopped
I hope to see my Pilot face to face	enjambed
When I have crossed the bar.	n/a

Finally, let's look in more detail at the sounds that Tennyson used.
First, notice that he used a lot of **alliteration**, but except for line two
where he used *clear call*, two words side-by-side and an adjective modifying
a noun, he did not alliterate words-side-by side. All of the other alliterations
are hidden by distance: *sunset-star, may-moaning, full-foam, drew-deep, flood-far*.
This lets the effect work on us, without our noticing it.

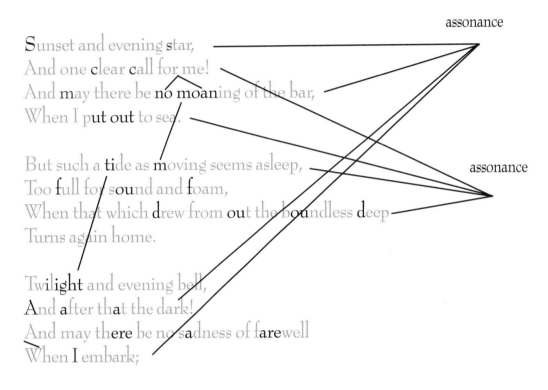

Notice something else that Tennyson did, something very subtle and quiet.
He used rhymes that were **assonance** with other rhymes. For example,
the first stanza has *me* and *sea*, and the second stanza has *asleep* and *deep*;
all four words share an assonance on the *e* sound. Then Tennyson did it again;
in the first stanza he used *star* and *bar*, and in the third stanza he used *dark*
and *embark*! And what about *bell* and *farewell*? The consonance on the *l* in these words
returns us to the key term of the first stanza: clear call.

If we didn't know how poets work, we might be tempted
to ask, "Did Tennyson really know he was doing all that?
Maybe that was just his style." Well, in partial answer to such
a question, let's look at part of his poem, "The Charge of the
Light Brigade" which he wrote in 1864 to memorialize the events in the
Battle of Balaclava, October 25, 1854. In that battle, as a result of a
mistake, 600 troops of the British light cavalry brigade staged a famous charge
against entrenched Turkish cannons, which massacred them. Here are the
first two stanzas:

Half a league, half a league,
Half a league onward,
All in the valley of Death
Rode the six hundred.
'Forward, the Light Brigade!
Charge for the guns!' he said:
Into the valley of Death
Rode the six hundred.

'Forward, the Light Brigade!'
Was there a man dismay'd?
Not tho' the soldier knew
Some one had blunder'd:
Their's not to make reply,
Their's not to reason why,
Their's but to do and die:
Into the valley of Death
Rode the six hundred.

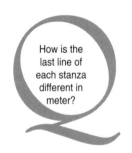

How is the last line of each stanza different in meter?

What we are seeing is a masterpiece of meter,
but not the same meter as in "Crossing the Bar." Instead of
iambs, "The Charge of the Light Brigade" is based on **dactyls**!
Remember, a dactyl is a three-syllable foot with the stress on the first.
Dactyls sound like DAdada DAdada; in fact, they sound like hoofbeats!
Some of the lines are perfect dactylic dimeter (two feet):

```
              1                 2
          Half a league,  /  half a league,
              1                 2
          'For ward, the  /  Light Bri gade!
              1                 2
          Charge for the  /  guns!' he said:
```

Other lines are dactylic, but have the last unstressed syllable dropped
off. When a final unstressed syllable is dropped from a line of dactylic
or trochaic meter, that is called **catalexis**:

```
              1                 2
          Half a league  /  on ward, ---
```

And in other lines, Tennyson follows the dactyls with a final stressed syllable
on a critical word; as though he had dropped the two remaining unstressed syllables!
Dadada Dadada BOOM.

```
              1               2               3
          All  in the  /  val ley of  /  Death --- ---
```

Nothing could be more different from "Crossing the Bar." We see different meters
for different themes—tranquil iambs and galloping dactyls.

But doesn't it take hours of hard work to get these poems into shape?
Are these poets really rewriting and rearranging lines and trying to
think of different words until they have every syllable in the poem
either stressed or not, according to some plan? Yes. They are.
Even in modern poetry, which often avoids regular meter, the poet
has to avoid regular meter *on purpose*. A poem is not a journal;
it is a finely crafted work of art. It is not just prose lines with rhymes
at the ends. Poetry is a high art.

We have taken close looks at a poem in iambic meter and a poem
in dactylic meter. Do poets write entire poems in anapestic meter?
Sometimes they do. The classic example is a love poem, "Afton Water," by the great
Scottish poet Robert Burns (1759-1796).

a small river in
Ayrshire

hillsides

Flow gently, sweet Afton, among thy green braes,
Flow gently, I'll sing thee a song in thy praise;
My Mary's asleep by thy murmuring stream,
Flow gently, sweet Afton, disturb not her dream.

Thou stock-dove, whose echo resounds thro' the glen,
Ye wild whistling blackbirds in yon thorny den,
Thou green-crested lapwing, thy screaming forbear,
I charge you disturb not my slumbering fair.

very small brook

How lofty, sweet Afton, thy neighbouring hills,
Far mark'd with the courses of clear winding rills;
There daily I wander as noon rises high,
My flocks and my Mary's sweet cot in my eye.

cottage

How pleasant thy banks and green valleys below,
Where wild in the woodlands the primroses blow;
There oft, as mild Ev'ning sweeps over the lea, — meadow
The sweet-scented birk shades my Mary and me.

— birch

Thy crystal stream, Afton, how lovely it glides,
And winds by the cot where my Mary resides, — wash
How wanton thy waters her snowy feet lave,
As gathering sweet flowrets she stems thy clear wave.

Flow gently, sweet Afton, among thy green braes,
Flow gently, sweet river, the theme of my lays; — poems
My Mary's asleep by thy murmuring stream,
Flow gently, sweet Afton, disturb not her dream.

In each quatrain, Burns uses four feet. The first is an iamb, and the last three are anapests. The result is a lilting, beautiful rhythm that suggests the playful movement of water down the stream.

1	2	3	4
Flow **gent** /	ly, sweet **Af** /	ton, a **mong** /	thy green **braes**,
iamb	anapest	anapest	anapest

1	2	3	4
Where **wild** /	in the **wood** /	lands the **prim** /	ro ses **blow**,
iamb	anapest	anapest	anapest

The magnificent exception to the perfect anapests comes in line eight, where Burns uses an **amphimacer** to give power (through an unanticipated double stress) to his warning:

1	2	3	4
I **charge** /	you dis **turb** /	**not** her **slum** /	ber ing **fair**.
iamb	anapest	amphimacer	anapest

53

The six-quatrain poem is filled with poetic genius. How did Burns
know to start with an iamb, rather than using four anapests?
We see that the poem is end-stopped in every line.
It has end rhyme throughout, with the first two lines
of each quatrain rhyming with each other, and the last two
lines of each quatrain rhyming with each other. In other
words, the rhyme scheme of the first quatrain is aabb. In the sixth
quatrain, Burns returns to his original rhyme scheme, bringing
the poem full circle.

It is a gentle, beautiful poem. Look at the soft consonants in the
first quatrain; as the lines say, they "flow gently":

> Flow gently, sweet Afton, among thy green braes,
> Flow gently, I'll sing thee a song in thy praise;
> My Mary's asleep by thy murmuring stream,
> Flow gently, sweet Afton, disturb not her dream.

We see beautiful combinations of alliteration and consonance on the *m*: *My Mary*
*m*ur*m*uring strea*m*, drea*m*. We also see the *ur* sound in *murmuring* and *disturb*,
and a host of *l*'s and *r*'s. In the second quatrain, Burns used *s*, *ds*, *st*, and *sk* sounds
to capture the whistle of the blackbirds and the screaming of the lapwings:

> Thou stock-dove, whose echo resounds thro' the glen,
> Ye wild whistling blackbirds in yon thorny den,
> Thou green-crested lapwing, thy screaming forbear,
> I charge you disturb not my slumbering fair.

The poem is filled, throughout, with sincerity and concern, a testament
to the ability of human beings to care about one another. And everyone
understood. When Robert Burns died, 10,000 people came to his
funeral, in an age when the speed of travel was three miles per hour.

The fourth traditional poetic foot is the **trochee**.
A trochee is an iamb in reverse, an anti-iamb. It is a two-syllable
foot with the stress on the first syllable.

Because English is naturally iambic, most poems are iambic
and iambs are often used for themes that are natural, noble, or positive.
Trochees, as anti-iambs that cancel out the normal iambic rhythm,
are the reverse. Often trochees suggest evil. Shakespeare used trochees
for the witches' chant in his tragedy *Macbeth*: "Double, double, toil and trouble,"
and William Blake used trochees to describe his scary, monstrous
tiger: "Tiger, tiger, burning bright..."

On the other hand, sometimes we find trochees that do not seem evil.
One great example is a carol about the king of Bohemia in the 10th Century,
King Wenceslas, who is famous for trying to feed the poor in his kingdom.
The carol is almost entirely in trochees, except that in many lines
the final unstressed syllable is dropped (this is called **catalexis**), which
results in a final stressed syllable, called a **masculine ending**.

Many lines have four trochees:

catalexis

<pre>
      1   2   3   4
When the / snow lay / round a / bout ---
      1   2   3   4
Bright ly / shone the / moon that / night ---
      1   2   3   4
When a / poor man / came in / sight ---
</pre>

Others have three:

<pre>
      1   2   3
Deep and / crisp and / e ven
      1   2   3
Un der / neath the / moun tain
</pre>

Why do trochees sound scary in one poem and not another?

Good King Wenceslas looked out
On the feast of Stephen
When the snow lay round about
Deep and crisp and even
Brightly shone the moon that night
Though the frost was cruel
When a poor man came in sight
Gath'ring winter fuel

"Hither, page, and stand by me
If thou know'st it, telling
Yonder peasant, who is he?
Where and what his dwelling?"
"Sire, he lives a good league hence
Underneath the mountain
Right against the forest fence
By Saint Agnes' fountain."

"Bring me flesh and bring me wine
Bring me pine logs hither
Thou and I will see him dine
When we bear him thither."
Page and monarch forth they went
Forth they went together
Through the rude wind's wild lament
And the bitter weather

1	2	3
Un der	neath the	moun tain

The masterpiece of **trochaic** poetry, however,
is one that we already mentioned, the great witches' chant
from Shakespeare's tragedy, *Macbeth*. In Act IV, scene 1,
we come upon three witches chanting up a revolting broth
of terrible trouble; here is the beginning:

Round about the cauldron go:
In the poisoned entrails throw.
Toad, that under cold stone   sweated
Days and nights has thirty-one
Sweltered venom sleeping got,
Boil thou first in the charmed pot.
Double, double toil and trouble;   from a swamp
Fire burn and cauldron bubble.   (fen)

Fillet of a fenny snake,
In the cauldron boil and bake;
Eye of newt and toe of frog,   a legless lizard
Wool of bat and tongue of dog,   owlet
Adder's fork and blindworm's sting,
Lizard's leg and howlet's wing.

Which of these two stanzas do you think is better?

Shakespeare used **trochaic tetrameter**, with **catalexis** to drop the
unstressed syllable from the fourth trochee; this allowed him both
to begin and end each line with a powerful stressed syllable.

1   2   3   4

In the / pois oned / en trails / throw ---

Notice that this also creates a series of double stresses, since the stressed syllable at
the end of each line is immediately followed by a stressed syllable at
the beginning of the next! In the last two lines, chanted by all the witches, Shakespeare
reverted to four complete trochees, leaving in the last unstressed syllable:

Doub le, / doub le / toil and / troub le;

Do you remember how Thomas Hardy used **stopped consonants** *P* and *B*, *T* and *D*, *K* and *G* to add power to his poem about the British navy practicing gunnery in the English Channel? Look at how Shakespeare, hundreds of years earlier, used these same consonants to enhance the scary harshness of the witches' voices:

> Round about the cauldron go:
> In the poisoned entrails throw.
> Toad, that under cold stone
> Days and nights has thirty-one
> Swelter'ded venom sleeping got,
> Boil thou first in the charmed pot.
> Double, double toil and trouble;
> Fire burn and cauldron bubble.
>
> Fillet of a fenny snake,
> In the cauldron boil and bake;
> Eye of newt and toe of frog,
> Wool of bat and tongue of dog,
> Adder's fork and blindworm's sting,
> Lizard's leg and howlet's wing.

P and B

T and D

K and G

Which pair sounds most explosive?

The blend of meter and sound is overwhelming, making us recoil in horror from the danger of the witches. Shakespeare was *so* talented, we see things in his poems that we rarely see in others. Look at lines three and four in the second stanza; do you see the *t and t-og* combination repeated:

> Eye of new**t and t**oe of fr**og**,
> Wool of ba**t and t**ongue of d**og**,

The closer we look, the more we see:

Round about the cauldron go:
In the poisoned entrails throw.
Toad, that under cold stone ————————> eye-rhyme
Days and nights has thirty-one
Sweltered venom sleeping got,
Boil thou first in the charmed pot.   end-stopped
Double, double toil and trouble;   end rhymes
Fire burn and cauldron bubble.   enhance the
                                        chanting effect

Fillet of a fenny snake,
In the cauldron boil and bake;
Eye of newt and toe of frog,   intense
Wool of bat and tongue of dog,   alliteration
Adder's fork and blindworm's sting,
Lizard's leg and howlet's wing.

Shakespeare was tricky! Look at Round and cauldron; poisoned and under; sweltered, thirty, first, burn, lizard, and blindworm. Look at the first line in the second stanza, about the slice of snake (*fillet*, which we would pronounce fiLAY, but is here pronounced FILLet). Do you hear the hissy, evil sound of the snake, with the bite of the *k*?

FFFillet oFFF a FFFenny SSSnake,

Do you hear the UBB, UBB, UBB, UBB drone at the end of the first stanza?
Or the OGG, OGG, EGG in *frog*, *dog*, *leg* in the second?
And all of this is worked into the stomping, trochaic chant:
DUNHduh DUNHduh DUNHduh DUNHduh....

FFFF

60

In examining these poems, we have mentioned terms such as **iambic pentameter** and **trochaic tetrameter**. Now that we have looked closely at the four main kinds of poetic foot—iamb, trochee, dactyl, and anapest— we can pause to look at the complete naming system for poetic lines.

We name a line of poetry for two things: the kind of foot it has and for the number of feet in the line. The numbers have their own designations:

monometer - one foot per line
dimeter - two feet per line
trimeter - three feet per line
tetrameter - four feet per line
pentameter - five feet per line
hexameter - six feet per line
heptameter - seven feet per line
octameter - eight feet per line

What if we did not have these words?

In other words, a line having *six dactyls* would be *dactylic hexameter*. A line having *four iambs* would be *iambic tetrameter*. Certain types of poems, as we will see, must be written in certain meters. For example, a **sonnet** must be written in iambic pentameter, with five iambs in each line. Notice that a line of **iambic pentameter** must, by definition, have **ten syllables**. Here is a couplet from one of Shakespeare's sonnets:

Not marble, nor the gilded monuments
Of princes shall outlive this powerful rhyme.

 1 2 3 4 5
Not **mar** / ble, **nor** / the **gil** / ded **mon** / u **ments**
 1 2 3 4 5
Of **prin** / ces, **shall** / out **live** / this **power** / ful **rhyme**

Each foot has two syllables. There are five feet. So there are ten syllables.

A line of **trochaic tetrameter** would have eight syllables, since it has four trochees of two syllables each. A line of **dactylic tetrameter** would have twelve syllables, each of the four dactyls having three:

1   2   3   4

Sud den ly / **some** one es / **caped** with my / **sax** o phone.

1   2   3   4   5   6   7   8   9   10   11   12

Anapestic trimeter would be three anapests, each one with three syllables, for a total of nine:

1   2   3

If you **go** / to the **moun** / tain, re **turn.**

1   2   3   4   5   6   7   8   9

And so on. A poem can employ any combination; there can be iambic dimeter, or trimeter, or tetrameter, or pentameter. Most common are the tetrameters and pentameters, with the very short lines and very long lines being far less typical. The most classic of lines is iambic pentameter, used in sonnets, but ballads, as we shall see, alternate iambic tetrameter and iambic trimeter!

A METER LAB

Let's write a poem with at least two stanzas (sections), and let's use a different meter in each stanza, trying to match the meter to what we are talking about. It might be fun to pick a photograph, and to write the poem as a companion to the photograph. An example:

Linville Gorge
Michael Clay Thompson

What happens to the meter in line four?

Boot heels crunching on the gravel,
Old dried oak leaves, snapping twigs and
In the frosty wind a hint of
Pine sap, then the gorge—the drop.

From here, the river seems a small affair,
A moving thread reflecting back the blue,
Descending from that mountain over there.
Ten thousand years, this gorge will still be here.

Even a mountain is evidence.
Even a tree in the morning sun.
Even the echoes in canyons can
Carry the whispers of rocks and winds.

The full length of my life is a moment, no more, to this gorge.
It was here all my years, and my father's and grandfather's, too.
It will be here millennia, thousands of years,
It is larger than I am, and older—and new.

For each of the lines on the following page assign a two-part answer, containing first a letter and then a number, according to this model:

i - iamb	3 - trimeter
t - trochee	4 - tetrameter
d - dactyl	5 - pentameter
a - anapest	6 - hexameter

If, for example, the line reads "Double, double, toil and trouble," your answer would be t4, meaning trochaic tetrameter. Why, because the line has four trochees:

1   2   3   4

dou ble / dou ble / toil and / trou ble

If the line were to read "The meaning of the text is plain to all," your answer would be i5, meaning iambic pentameter. ·

1   2   3   4   5

The mean / ing of / the text / is plain / to all

If it were "At the top of the Hindenberg no one arrived," your answer would be a4, anapestic tetrameter.

1   2   3   4

At the top / of the Hin / den berg no / one ar rived.

And if it were "Suddenly everyone gathered the" your answer would be d3, meaning dactylic trimeter.

1   2   3

Sud den ly / ev ery one / gath ered the

1. The crowd dispersed as officers approached.
2. Officers approached us slowly.
3. I saw the officer.
4. As we saw the ship arriving...
5. At the back of the room was a boy.
6. Suddenly someone collected the settlement.
7. If I profane with my unworthiest hand...
8. I never saw a purple cow
9. The mind makes all the difference.
10. Crusty crabs and barnacles were...
11. If I thought you would ask I would laugh.
12. Never a moment to fasten a halibut.
13. After laughter, rafter.
14. It is hoped that the fallible person will ask.
15. Munching cinders, certain senders.
16. Why did he celebrate having a sensible...
17. I ask because I want to know.
18. Hurricanes crowded the churning Atlantic and...
19. On the freighter the crew looked around at the sea.
20. Pounding drumbeats rocked the valley.
21. Make the gruel thick and slab.
22. 'Tis now the very witching time of night.
23. I will, my lord.
24. The time is out of joint. O cursèd spite...
25. Within the book and volume of my brain...
26. The bee is not afraid of me.
27. On whose forbidden ear...
28. Come see the north wind's masonry.
29. The woodland paths are dry.
30. Teach the free man how to praise the...
31. In the importance and noise of tomorrow we...
32. And your hair has become very white.
33. The moon was shining sulkily.

5

stanza

Poems are often divided into similar sections, called *stanzas*.

The word *stanza* comes from the Italian word that means "room."

The stanzas of a poem are like the rooms of a house.

Sometimes, stanzas are named for the number of lines that they contain:

How is a poem stanza similar to a room?

couplet: a two-line stanza

triplet: a three-line stanza, also called a *tercet*

quatrain: a four-line stanza

quintet: a five-line stanza, also called a *quinquain*

sestet: a six-line stanza

septet: a seven-line stanza

octet: an eight-line stanza

HEROIC COUPLET

Within these general stanza forms there are variations, such as the **heroic** (also called *closed*) **couplet**. Heroic couplets are couplets that rhyme, written in iambic pentameter. In 1709 Alexander Pope wrote a long poem, called "An Essay on Criticism," in heroic couplets. Here is the beginning:

> 'Tis hard to say if greater want of skill
> Appear in writing or in judging ill,
> But of the two less dangerous is the offense
> To tire our patience than mislead our sense
> Some few in that but numbers err in this,
> Ten censure wrong for one who writes amiss,
> A fool might once himself alone expose,
> Now one in verse makes many more in prose.

We see four heroic couplets. Do you see that the lines are iambic pentameter?

$$1 \qquad 2 \qquad 3 \qquad 4 \qquad 5$$

'Tis **hard** / to **say** / if **great** / er **want** / of **skill**

TERZA RIMA

There is also a special form of **triplet**, called **terza rima**. Terza rima
is a three-line stanza, usually iambic pentameter, in which the first
and third lines of each stanza rhyme, and the middle line becomes
the beginning rhyme of the next stanza. The most famous poem
written in terza rima is Percy Shelley's "Ode to the West Wind," which begins:

O WILD West Wind, thou breath of Autumn's being—	a
Thou from whose unseen presence the leaves dead	b
Are driven, like ghosts from an enchanter fleeing,	a
Yellow, and black, and pale, and hectic red,	b
Pestilence-stricken multitudes!—O thou	c
Who chariotest to their dark wintry bed	b
The wingèd seeds, where they lie cold and low,	c
Each like a corpse within its grave, until	d
Thine azure sister of the Spring shall blow	c
Her clarion o'er the dreaming earth, and fill	d
(Driving sweet buds like flocks to feed in air)	e
With living hues and odours plain and hill—	d
Wild Spirit, which art moving everywhere—	e
Destroyer and Preserver—hear, O hear!	f

Do you see how the middle line of each triplet rhymes becomes the
first and last rhymes of the next triplet? Shelley does not stick strictly
to iambic pentameter, but the poem is roughly that:

$$\begin{array}{ccccc} 1 & 2 & 3 & 4 & 5 \end{array}$$

De **stroy** / er **and** / Pre **ser** / ver // **hear** / O **hear**!

Notice the **caesura** in the last line. We indicate a caesura
with the double slash //. This caesura comes in the middle of the fourth iamb!

VILLANELLE

If you think that terza rima would be difficult to write
(it is, it is), wait until you see the villanelle!
A villanelle is a poem of nineteen lines: five tercets and a quatrain.
There are only two rhymes in a villanelle!
All of the tercets rhyme aba, and the quatrain rhymes abaa,
so the poem is aba aba aba aba aba abaa.
To make it more complicated, lines 6, 12, and 18 repeat
line one, and lines 9, 15, and 19 repeat line 3!
There is no specified meter for a villanelle.
If we wanted to write a playful villanelle, we might write
something like this:

1: 6, 12, 18
3: 9, 15, 19

The M&M's were scattered on the floor.	a
My startled brain decayed without delay.	b
I stood, and walked directly through the door.	a
I thought I couldn't take it any more.	a
I'd wanted M&M's all day;	b
The M&M's were scattered on the floor.	a
My mind degenerated to a roar.	a
I'd buy more M&M's, but couldn't pay.	b
I stood, and walked directly through the door.	a
I'd never dropped my M&M's before.	a
I wanted just to stand and walk away.	b
The M&M's were scattered on the floor.	a
To see the candy chaos made me sore.	a
The colors spread across: a sad array.	b
I stood, and walked directly through the door.	a
The horror of the scene I could not ignore.	a
An M here, M there, M's galore, astray...	b
The M&M's were scattered on the floor.	a
I stood, and walked directly through the door.	a

BALLAD

Although the triplet-based **terza rima** and the **villanelle** are fun,
and are not extremely rare, they are nonetheless not typical forms.
Far more common than the **triplet** is the **quatrain**, the four-line stanza.
Many poems are made of quatrains, in the abab rhyming pattern,
and one variation of the quatrain, the **ballad** stanza, is among
the most important and popular of all stanza forms in English poetry.
The ballad consists of alternating lines of **iambic tetrameter**
and **iambic trimeter**, rhyming abcb. In other words, the second
and fourth lines rhyme, but the first and third do not.

In American poetry, the genius of the ballad is Emily Dickinson.
In her poem "LXXIII," she used two ballad stanzas to communicate
how illusory life's solutions can be:

> I many times thought peace had come,
> When peace was far **away**;
> As wrecked men deem they sight the land
> At centre of the **sea**,
>
> And struggle slacker, but to prove,
> As hopelessly as **I**,
> How many the fictitious shores
> Before the harbor **lie**.

less

ly

Notice the **near rhyme** of *away* and *sea*
in the first stanza.

The inner structures of poems sometimes remind
us of the perfect structures we see in nature
such as the molecular structure of crystals such as salt.

In a different poem, Dickinson wrote this ballad stanza,
that uses **consonance** rather than rhyme in lines two and four.
We are almost tempted to think that this is a case of **apophany**,
but it is not quite. Remember, apophany is when two consonants are the same,
but the vowel between them is different. The words *wake* and *week*
would be apophany.

'Twas later when the summer went
Than when the cricket **came**,
And yet we knew that gentle clock
Meant nought but going **home**.

In the ballad, lines of iambic tetrameter such as this one:

1   2   3   4

'Twas **la** / ter **when** / the **sum** / mer **went**

alternate with lines of iambic trimeter such as this one:

1   2   3

Than **when** / the **crick** / et **came**

/ ter **when** /

Samuel Taylor Coleridge used the ballad stanza for his
masterpiece, "The Rime of the Ancient Mariner." Here are
three stanzas describing the ship stuck at sea in a burning, dead calm:

All in a hot and copper sky,
The bloody Sun, at **noon**,
Right up above the mast did stand,
No bigger than the **Moon**.

Day after day, day after day,
We stuck, nor breath nor **motion**;
As idle as a painted ship
Upon a painted **ocean**.

Water, water, everywhere,
And all the boards did **shrink**;
Water, water, everywhere,
Nor any drop to **drink**.

Which of these stanzas do you like most?

Notice that in the famous third stanza, Coleridge varied from the normal
iambic tetrameter in lines one and three, briefly shifting into **trochees**
to give power to the words, and using **catalexis** to drop the final unstressed
syllable in the fourth trochee.

Wa ter / wa ter / ev ery / where

In 1789 William Blake used, not the ballad stanza, but a
different form of quatrain, to create the introduction
to his *Songs of Innocence*. The poem, mostly trochaic, is five quatrains long:

Piping down the valleys wild,   a
Piping songs of pleasant glee,   b
On a cloud I saw a child,   a
And he laughing said to me: b

"Pipe a song about a lamb!"   c
So I piped with merry cheer.   d
"Piper, pipe that song again";   c
So I piped: he wept to hear.   d

"Drop thy pipe, thy happy pipe   e
Sing thy songs of merry cheer":   d
So I sung the same again,   c
While he wept with joy to hear.   d

"Piper sit thee down and write   f
In a book that all may read."   g
So he vanished from my sight,   f
And I plucked a hollow reed,   g

And I made a rural pen,   h
And I stained the water clear,   d
And I wrote my happy songs   i
Every child may joy to hear.   d

Why is
the child
on a
cloud?

76

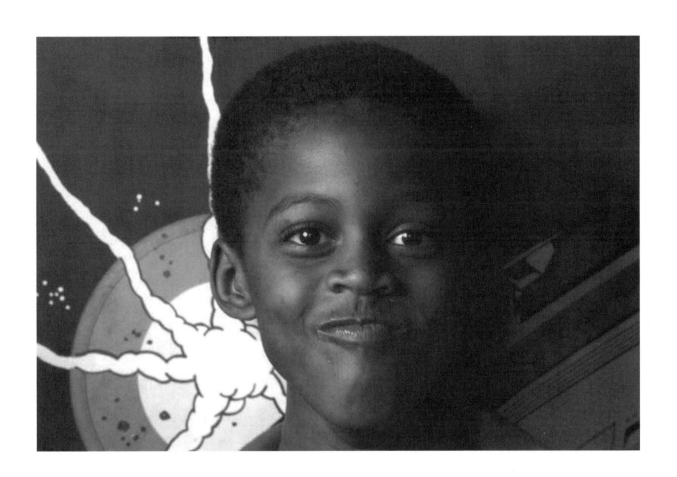

William Butler Yeats wrote this poem in 1899.
It has eight lines, but you can see that it is really
made of two quatrains, in which Yeats used repetition
rather than rhyme:

He Wishes for the Cloths of Heaven
William Butler Yeats

Had I the heavens' embroidered cloths,
Enwrought with golden and silver light,
The blue and the dim and the dark cloths
Of night and light and the half-light,
I would spread the cloths under your feet:
But I, being poor, have only my dreams;
I have spread my dreams under your feet;
Tread softly because you tread upon my dreams.

What is
the best line
in this poem?
Why?

The poem is roughly **iambic**, with rhyme scheme abab cdcd: *cloths light cloths light feet dreams feet dreams*. We see **alliteration** in a compound adjective, *dim and the dark*, and we see **internal rhyme**, *Of night and light*, *spread* and *tread*. We see inversions of sounds: *dreams spread*. There is **assonance** in *cloths* and *enwrought*. The poem is **end-stopped** and uses a **caesura** to emphasize "being poor."

QUINTET

A five-line stanza is a quintet. Perhaps the most famous poem
to employ a quintet variation is Percy Shelley's (1792-1822) "Ode to a Skylark"
which expresses Shelley's almost childlike joy with the world.
The poem contains twenty-one quintets; here are the first two:

> Hail to thee, blithe spirit!
> Bird thou never wert —
> That from heaven or near it
> Pourest thy full heart
> In profuse strains of unpremeditated art.

How would you describe the spirit of this poem?

> Higher still and higher
> From the earth thou springest,
> Like a cloud of fire;
> The blue deep thou wingest,
> And singing still dost soar, and soaring ever singest.

LIMERICK

Another important quintet form is the limerick. A limerick is a five-line
nonsense poem, mostly in **anapest**, with a rhyme scheme aabba.
Lines one, two, and five have three feet, but lines three and four have only two feet.
Limericks have only one stanza; poets don't usually write a poem of three or five limerick
stanzas, and in fact, the limerick has not been used as a stanza for major poetry, but more
for light, comic, humorous poems. Here is a limerick by W.S. Gilbert, which was put
to music by his partner, Sir Arthur Sullivan, and performed in their 1877 play *The
Sorcerer*:

> Oh, my name is John Wellington Wells,
> I'm a dealer in magic and spells,
> In blessings and curses,
> And ever-filled purses,
> In prophecies, witches and knells.

Even though the limerick is not, in one sense, a stanza used
in serious poetry, it nevertheless employs serious techniques. Let's
look more closely. First notice the aabba rhyme scheme of end-stopped
end rhymes:

Oh, my name is John Wellington Wells,	a
I'm a dealer in magic and spells,	a
In blessings and curses,	b
And ever-filled purses,	b
In prophecies, witches and knells.	a

Then examine the meter closely. We see perfect anapests! Remember
that an anapest is a three-syllable foot with the stress on the third syllable.

        1   2   3
Oh, my name / is John Wel / lington Wells,

        1   2   3
I'm a dea / ler in ma / gic and spell

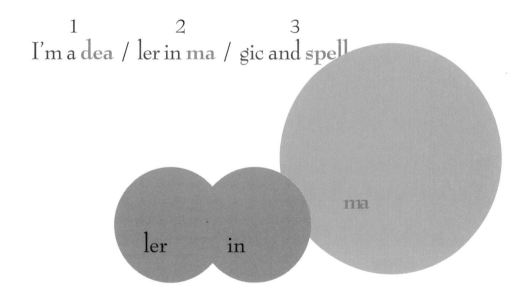

Did you notice the combination of masculine and feminine rhyme?
How does the meter change in lines three and four?

SESTET

A sestet is a six-line stanza. William Cowper (1731-1800) used sestets in his poem "The Castaway," about a man washed overboard in a storm at sea. The poem contains eleven sestets; here are the first four. *Albion* is an old name of England:

> Obscurest night involved the sky,
>   The Atlantic billows roared,
> When such a destined wretch as I,
>   Washing headlong from on board,
> Of friends, of hope, of all bereft,
> His floating home forever left.
>
> No braver chief could Albion boast
>   Than he with whom he went,
> Nor ever ship left Albion's coast,
>   With warmer wishes sent.
> He loved them both, but both in vain,
> Nor him beheld, nor her again.
>
> Not long beneath the whelming brine,
>   Expert to swim, he lay;
> Nor soon he felt his strength decline,
>   Or courage die away;
> But waged with death a lasting strife,
> Supported by despair of life.
>
> He shouted: nor his friends had failed
>   To check the vessel's course,
> But so the furious blast prevailed,
>   That, pitiless perforce,
> They left their outcast mate behind,
> And scudded still before the wind.

Q Which of these four stanzas do you like most?

Cowper's sestets are like ballad stanzas with heroic couplets added to the ends! Do you see the **eye-rhyme** in the last two lines?

RIME ROYAL

A seven-line stanza is a **septet**, and one of the most famous
forms of septet, rarely used now but once popular, is **rime royal**,
or **rhyme royal**. The rime royal stanza has seven lines of iambic pentameter,
rhyme scheme ababbcc. Rime Royal was introduced into English poetry
by Geoffrey Chaucer (1340-1400) and became known as *royal*
after King James I of Scotland favored it. Rime Royal went out of fashion
in the 17th century. Here is the first rime royal stanza from Thomas
Wyatt, the Elder's (1503-1542) poem "They Flee from Me."

They flee from me that sometime did me seek	a
With naked foot stalking in my chamber.	b
I have seen them gentle tame and meek	a
That now are wild and do not remember	b
That sometime they put themselves in danger	b
To take bread at my hand; and now they range	c
Busily seeking with a continual change.	c

Thomas Wyatt's life was dramatic. He held numerous important posts
but was imprisoned in the Tower of London twice, the first time for
quarreling with the Duke of Suffolk. While in the Tower, Wyatt witnessed
the execution of Anne Boleyn on May 19, 1536. We see in this septet
Wyatt's feeling of abandonment by his friends, whom he compares to birds.

Notice how powerful an effect Wyatt created by **enjambing** his lines; the poem
feels like a confession or comment, rather than a poem. You hardly notice
the end rhymes because there is no pause on *meek*, *remember*, *danger*,
or *range*; the poem reads right through those words, causing them to
recede into the background and allowing the ideas to move forward.
Enjambed poems have a very different feel from **end-stopped** poems.

Even though our interest in the rime royal stanza is largely scholarly
since modern poets rarely employ it, the form is nonetheless
interesting and important to know about.

OCTET

An octet is an eight-line stanza. As we have seen,
poets have used enormous creative variation in making
their stanzas. A poem may be a quatrain, but be iambic.
Or it may be trochaic. Or anapestic. It may have end rhyme,
or not. It may be end-stopped or enjambed. The octet
is no different. There are many different ways to write
an octet. Among the most famous poems to use the octet
is Robert Burns's poem, written in 1795, asserting the
equality and dignity of the average person. Called
"For A' That and A' That" (For All That and All That)
the poem, which may have been inspired by Thomas
Paine's *Rights of Man*, contains five octets, or forty lines.

How is an octet different from two quatrains?

Though very great, the poem is challenging for us to read today
because Burns defiantly wrote the poem in regional Scottish
dialect, which was despised by the English.

"So what if we're poor?" Burns asks. Do not hang
your head like a coward. Do not be ashamed.
So what if we dine on homely fare, or wear coarse woolen cloth
(hodden gray), or toil obscurely? It is the man, not
the rank, that is the gold (gowd). So what if some young
fellow (birkie) is called a lord, and struts around with ribbons
and stars on his chest? We don't need those tinsel shows.
The man of independent mind laughs at that. The honest
man is king of men. So what if someone is a knight,
or a prince, a marquis, or a duke? An honest man,
with sense and worth, has a higher rank. And the day
is coming when, over all the world, all men will be
brothers. A man is a man, for all that.

You should be able to make out most of the sentences with the help of context,
but just in case: hings-hangs, an'-and, gowd-gold, hamely-homely,
gie-give, e'er-ever, sae-so, birkie-brisk fellow, ca'd-called, wha-what, cuif-dolt,
ribband-ribbon, mak-make, aboon-above, guid-good, mauna fa-must not claim,
pith-essence, o'-of, a'-all, bear the gree-win the prize, gree-prize, o'er-over,
brithers-brothers. A guinea was a gold coin worth only twenty-one shillings.

For a' that

Robert Burns

Is there for honest poverty
That hings his head, an' a' that?
The coward slave, we pass him by—
We dare be poor for a' that!
For a' that, an' a' that!
Our toils obscure, an' a' that,
The rank is but the guinea's stamp,
The man's the gowd for a' that.

What though on hamely fare we dine,
Wear hodding grey, an' a' that?
Gie fools their silks, and knaves their wine—
A man's a man for a' that.
For a' that, an' a' that,
Their tinsel show, an' a' that,
The honest man, tho e'er sae poor,
Is king o' men for a' that.

Ye see yon birkie ca'd 'a lord,'
Wha struts, an' stares, an' a' that?
Tho hundreds worship at his word,
He's but a cuif for a' that.
For a' that, an' a' that,
His ribband, star, an' a' that,
The man o' independent mind,
He looks an' laughs at a' that.

A prince can mak a belted knight,
A marquis, duke, an' a' that!
But an honest man's aboon his might -
Guid faith, he mauna fa' that!
For a' that, an' a' that,
Their dignities, an' a' that,
The pith o' sense an pride o' worth,
Are higher rank than a' that.

Then let us pray that come it may
(As come it will for a' that),
That Sense and Worth o'er a' the earth,
Shall bear the gree an' a' that.
For a' that, an' a' that,
It's coming yet for a' that,
That man to man, the world o'er
Shall brithers be for a' that.

Which stanza is most inspiring?

We will show the poem again on the next page to assist discussion.

Is there for honest poverty
That hings his head, an' **a' that**?
The coward slave, we pass him by—
We dare be poor **for a' that**!
For a' that, an' **a' that**!
Our toils obscure, an' **a' that**,
The rank is but the guinea's stamp,
The man's the gowd **for a' that**.

What though on hamely fare we dine,
Wear hodding grey, an' **a' that**?
Gie fools their silks, and knaves their wine—
A man's a man **for a' that**.
For a' that, an' **a' that**,
Their tinsel show, an' **a' that**,
The honest man, tho e'er sae poor,
Is king o' men **for a' that**.

Ye see yon birkie ca'd 'a lord,'
Wha struts, an' stares, an' **a' that**?
Tho hundreds worship at his word,
He's but a cuif **for a' that**.
For a' that, an' **a' that**,
His ribband, star, an' **a' that**,
The man o independent mind,
He looks an' laughs at **a' that**.

A prince can mak a belted knight,
A marquis, duke, an' **a' that**!
But an honest man's aboon his might -
Guid faith, he mauna fa' **that**!
For a' that, an' **a' that**,
Their dignities, an' **a' that**,
The pith o' sense an pride o' worth,
Are higher rank than **a' that**.

Then let us pray that come it may
(As come it will **for a' that**),
That Sense and Worth o'er a' the earth,
Shall bear the gree an' **a' that**.
For a' that, an' **a' that**,
It's coming yet **for a' that**,
That man to man, the world o'er
Shall brithers be **for a' that**.

brithers

For *all that*, for all the problems of poverty, and all tinsel
of aristocracy, a man is just a man. An equal. Burns had
the ability to write the poem in standard English, but the dialect was
part of his message: we Scots are the equal of you English.
There is no reason to write in your dialect; ours is just as good.

Notice that the last four lines of each octet are a kind of chorus, not
word for word, but beginning with the same fifth line, and ending with
a' that in lines five, six, and eight. Did you see the pretty internal rhyme
in the first octet: *poor obscure*? We begin to feel the imperative of the stanza;
Burns *needed eight lines* to develop each idea.

88

SONNET

All of the stanza forms we have seen are important, but few of them have played as important a role in the history of poetry as the **sonnet**, *little song* in Italian. The sonnet, a fourteen-line poem of iambic pentameter, is a major stanza form in English poetry; it has been used by many poets and is the form of some of the most important poems in the language, including a famous series of sonnets by William Shakespeare.

Sir Thomas Wyatt (1503-1542) first introduced the sonnet into English poetry; he used the form called the Italian or Petrarchan (after Francesco Petrarch, Italian poet, 1304-1374) sonnet. Henry Howard (the Earl of Surrey) and William Shakespeare later developed the English form of the sonnet. The sonnet is usually the entire poem of fourteen lines, but there is also a form known as the **sonnet redoublé**, consisting of fifteen sonnets in which the fifteenth stanza repeats lines from each of the first fourteen! Poets such as Shakespeare and T.S. Eliot have also hidden sonnets longer works; this is called a **submerged** sonnet. There are several different kinds of sonnets that are important in English poetry:

ITALIAN (PETRARCHAN)
abbaabba cdecde

The Italian sonnet breaks into **an octave and a sestet**.
The rhyme scheme of the octave is usually abba abba,
and the sestet is usually cde cde but these forms vary often.
The Italian sonnet develops a problem in the octave,
and then turns (this is called a *volta*) and resolves it in the sestet.

ENGLISH (SHAKESPEAREAN)
abab cdcd efef gg

The English sonnet breaks into **three quatrains and a couplet**,
ababcdcdefefgg. The English sonnet may introduce
a problem in the first quatrain, make it more complicated
in the next two quatrains, and then solve it in the final couplet.

What do these three have in common?

SPENSERIAN
abab bcbc cdcd ee

The Spenserian sonnet is a variation of the English sonnet that Edmund Spenser developed; it connects the quatrains by repeating rhymes, rather than beginning new rhymes in each quatrain.
The Spenserian sonnet has not been widely used, but it shows us that within the sonnet form there are interesting variations possible.

Among the crown jewels of English poetry are the 154 sonnets of William Shakespeare, which reach a grace and depth unmatched by any other collection. Many of them are love poems, as sonnets often are, and many of them form a sequence, one sonnet seeming to be a continuation of the sonnet before it. Here is sonnet 76:

Why is my verse so barren of new pride,	a
So far from variation or quick change?	b
Why with the time do I not glance aside	a
To new-found methods and to compounds strange?	b
Why write I still all one, ever the same,	c
And keep invention in a noted weed*,	d
That every word doth almost tell my name,	c
Showing their birth and where they did proceed?	d
O, know, sweet love, I always write of you,	e
And you and love are still my argument;	f
So all my best is dressing old words new,	e
Spending again what is already spent:	f
For as the sun is daily new and old,	g
So is my love still telling what is told.	g

"Why are all my poems alike," Shakespeare asks? Because they are all about you.
We see that this sonnet by Shakespeare is, not surprisingly, a Shakespearean sonnet, made of three quatrains and a couplet. The solution of the poem lies in the couplet. Shakespeare does not adhere absolutely to a perfect pattern of iambics, but the sonnet is based on the feeling of iambic pentameter, and many lines are perfect iambic pentameter:

```
       1           2          3         4          5
O know / sweet love  // I al / ways write / of you
```

Notice that the poem is entirely end-stopped, with masculine end rhymes throughout. Do you see the assonance of *Why, time,* and *aside*, and of *best* and *dressing*, and of *spending* and *again*? Of *showing, O, know, noted, told, old*? Shakespeare was adept at subtle song. Notice the effective caesura in line nine, indicated by the // in the scan above.

*A "noted weed" means well-known clothes.

Although it is easy to love such a touching poem,
the key thing for our purposes is to perceive the form clearly,
so that we will recognize any English sonnet when we see it.
An English sonnet is three quatrains and a couplet:

Why is my verse so barren of new pride,   a
So far from variation or quick change?   b
Why with the time do I not glance aside   a
To new-found methods and to compounds strange?   b

Why write I still all one, ever the same,   c
And keep invention in a noted weed,   d
That every word doth almost tell my name,   c
Showing their birth and where they did proceed?   d

O, know, sweet love, I always write of you,   e
And you and love are still my argument;   f
So all my best is dressing old words new,   e
Spending again what is already spent: f

For as the sun is daily new and old,   g
So is my love still telling what is told.   g

Look at the beautiful sounds and soft consonants in "O, know, sweet love,
I always write of you."

Which of these are the "soft" consonants?

A SUBMERGED SONNET

Undoubtedly, the greatest submerged sonnet in English literature comes from William Shakespeare.

In Act I, scene 5 of his play *Romeo and Juliet*, which was written entirely in poetry, Shakespeare submerged a sonnet in the lines of the play. The flow of dialogue is so natural, the sonnet could easily go unnoticed. But this scene is the meeting of the two lovers, and Shakespeare used the power of the sonnet, a traditional form for love poetry, to enhance the meeting.

In the scene, Romeo has gone to a party at the Capulet's, a family that is involved in a blood feud with his family, the Montagues. He should not even be there, but he is, and he is discovered by Tybalt, a man of the Capulet family who wants to attack him and drive him away. Old Capulet, Juliet's father, tells Tybalt to leave Romeo alone. We watch as Romeo, for the first time, spots Juliet, and is instantly in love. The witty dialogue between the two shows us that they are a perfect match for each other.

Now that we know what a sonnet is, we can detect the sonnet hiding there. Here is part of the play, with the sonnet revealed. Notice how Shakespeare skillfully splits the sonnet up between Romeo and Juliet, concealing the structure. Romeo speaks all of the first quatrain, Juliet all of the second, and the third quatrain and couplet are divided between them; with the two coming together to complete the final couplet.

Q Why is this called submerged? Is that a good term?

Act I, v.

94

CAPULET: Go to, go to;
You are a saucy boy: is't so, indeed?
This trick may chance to scathe you. I know what:
You must contrary me! Marry, 'tis time.—
Well said, my hearts!—You are a princox; go:
Be quiet, or—More light, more light!—For shame!
I'll make you quiet.—What, cheerly, my hearts!

TYBALT: Patience perforce with wilful choler meeting
Makes my flesh tremble in their different greeting.
I will withdraw, but this intrusion shall
Now seeming sweet convert to bitter gall.   *Exit*

ROMEO [To JULIET]: If I profane with my unworthiest hand
This holy shrine, the gentle sin is this:
My lips, two blushing pilgrims, ready stand
To smooth that rough touch with a tender kiss.

JULIET: Good pilgrim, you do wrong your hand too much,
Which mannerly devotion shows in this;
For saints have hands that pilgrims' hands do touch,
And palm to palm is holy palmers' kiss.

ROMEO: Have not saints lips, and holy palmers too?

JULIET: Ay, pilgrim, lips that they must use in prayer.

ROMEO: O, then, dear saint, let lips do what hands do;
They pray—grant thou, lest faith turn to despair.

JULIET: Saints do not move, though grant for prayers' sake.

ROMEO: Then move not, while my prayer's effect I take.
Thus from my lips, by yours, my sin is purged.

JULIET: Then have my lips the sin that they have took.

ROMEO: Sin from thy lips? O trespass sweetly urged!
Give me my sin again.

After Shakespeare, William Wordsworth (1770-1850) is widely regarded as the greatest sonnet writer in English poetry. In 1843 he explained in a letter to his friend Samuel Taylor Coleridge what had been on his mind when he wrote, in 1802, a sonnet entitled "Written in London, September, 1802."

"This was written immediately after my return from France to London, when I could not but be struck, as here described, with the vanity and parade of our own country, especially in great towns and cities, as contrasted with the quiet, and I may say the desolation, that the Revolution had produced in France. This must be borne in mind, or else the reader may think that in this and the succeeding sonnets I have exaggerated the mischief engendered and fostered among us by undisturbed wealth"

Wordsworth's sonnet:

O Friend! I know not which way I must look	a
For comfort, being, as I am, opprest,	b
To think that now our life is only drest	b
For show; mean handy-work of craftsman, cook,	a
Or groom! — We must run glittering like a brook	a
In the open sunshine, or we are unblest:	b
The wealthiest man among us is the best:	b
No grandeur now in nature or in book	a
Delights us. Rapine, avarice, expense,	c
This is idolatry; and these we adore:	d
Plain living and high thinking are no more:	d
The homely beauty of the good old cause	e
Is gone; our peace, our fearful innocence,	c
And pure religion breathing household laws.	e

How would you compare the ideas of this sonnet to those in Robert Burns's poem, "A Man's a Man for A' That"?

If we compare Wordsworth's rhyme scheme to the other three
sonnet variations we have encountered, we see that it is a form
of the Italian or Petrarchan sonnet. Like an Italian sonnet,
it is composed of an octet and a sestet, but the sestet is different.
Wordsworth's rhyme scheme is:

abbaabba cddece
octet   sestet

Review below the things we learned about Italian, English, and Spenserian
sonnets, and you can easily see that Wordsworth was using the first.

ITALIAN (PETRARCHAN) abbaabba cdecde
The Italian sonnet breaks into **an octave and a sestet**.
The rhyme scheme of the octave is usually abba abba,
and **the sestet is usually cde cde but these forms vary often.**
The Italian sonnet develops a problem in the octave,
and then turns (this is called a *volta*) and resolves it in the sestet.

ENGLISH (SHAKESPEAREAN) abab cdcd efef gg
The English sonnet breaks into **three quatrains and a couplet**,
ababcdcdefefgg. The English sonnet may introduce
a problem in the first quatrain, make it more complicated
in the next two quatrains, and then solve it in the final couplet.

SPENSERIAN abab bcbc cdcd ee
The Spenserian sonnet is a variation of the English sonnet that
Edmund Spenser developed; it interlocks the sonnet's three
quatrains' rhymes, rather than moving to new rhymes in each quatrain.
The Spenserian sonnet has not been widely used, but it shows us that
within the sonnet form there are interesting variations possible.

A STANZA LAB—WRITING

Let's write a poem in one of the stanza forms we have studied. Find a photograph of an intriguing person, someone who has an expressive face, someone who is very different from you, and yet someone you can identify with in some way. Then write a poem from that person's point of view, as you imagine it might be, using one of our stanza forms. You might experiment with enjambed lines that suppress the end rhymes and make the poem sound more like prose. Try using a spondee rather than one of the iambs in order to emphasize something important.

Chen's Sonnet
Michael Clay Thompson

The soil is black here on my farm, and I
can see the Yellow River far below
the slope as I begin to plow. I try
to keep the furrows straight. You know,
we raised five children here; they live across
the valley now. I never see them, or
not often, yet I sometimes feel their thoughts
arriving with the wind. I have two more
grandchildren since the rains fell in the spring,
I've never seen them. I had hoped I could,
but now the drought is killing everything
and I must work, start early. Work is good;
It takes my thoughts away from what I miss—
her face, her smile, those eyes, the whole list.

In 1916 William Butler Yeats wrote this poem, entitled "To a Friend Whose Work Has Come to Nothing." You see that Yeats used a combination of end-stopped and enjambed end rhyme to compose four quatrains, mostly in iambic trimeter. He used a number of near rhymes, rather than perfect rhymes, to give a more candid feeling to the poem. Be secret, Yeats says twice.

There are two questions that offer valuable discussions, relative to this poem. First, are the ideas in this poem similar to those in Burns's poem, "A Man's a Man," and to the ideas in Wordsworth's London sonnet, or are they different? Which of the two previous poems is most similar to this one by Yeats?

The second question is—and it is a challenging question with no certain answer—Why did Yeats use four quatrains for this poem, rather than a sonnet? The poem is very close to the number of lines in a sonnet. Why did Yeats choose the fourth quatrain, rather than a couplet at that point? And why did he prefer iambic trimeter here to the iambic pentameter that is standard in a sonnet?

Now all the truth is out,	a
Be secret and take defeat	b
From any brazen throat,	a
For how can you compete,	b
Being honour bred, with one	c
Who, were it proved he lies,	d
Were neither shamed in his own	c
Nor in his neighbours' eyes?	d
Bred to a harder thing	e
Than Triumph, turn away	f
And like a laughing string	e
Whereon mad fingers play	f
Amid a place of stone,	c
Be secret and exult,	g
Because of all things known	c
That is most difficult.	g

A STANZA LAB

DISCUSSION

George Gordon (1788-1824), also known as Lord Byron, was one of the greatest poetic geniuses in English poetry. Born with a club foot, he was nonetheless dashing and handsome, and was the center of a cult of admiration for his heroic and romantic poems. Deciding that action was as important as words, Byron sailed to aid the Greeks in their fight for freedom from the Ottoman Turks, and he died in Missolonghi, Greece, in 1824. His body was sent to England, where both Westminster and St. Paul's cathedral refused to accept it; it was then placed in a family vault in Nottinghamshire. He had been the most widely read poet of his time, and had written the poem below in November of 1820. The question for us is, what is the stanza form of this poem? What is the meter? (We obviously see two quatrains; but, for example, are these limericks? Or not? Why did Byron use humor in a poem about such strong ideas?)

When a man hath no freedom to fight for at home,
Let him combat for that of his neighbours;
Let him think of the glories of Greece and of Rome,
And get knock'd on the head for his labours,

To do good to mankind is the chivalrous plan,
And is always as nobly requited;
Then battle for freedom wherever you can,
And, if not shot or hang'd, you'll get knighted.

What is your favorite line in this poem?

102

6

figures of speech

Poets can shape the sounds of poems in many ways.
They create patterns of sound through rhyme, alliteration, assonance,
and consonance. They shape the rise and fall of stressed and
unstressed syllables, creating meters that move with the thoughts of the poem.
And they shape the lines of poems into groups, making larger
structures that allow ideas to be developed in beautiful ways.

But in addition to all of these techniques for composing the sounds
of poems, poets also have special ways of shaping ideas.

It is an odd fact of language that a direct statement
about something often fails to capture the life of the thing, fails
to communicate its essence. If we try to say, about an asphalt road in the summer,
that "It was hot," or even "It was really hot," the idea is flat.
But if we say, "My feet on the asphalt felt like bacon sizzling in the pan!"
then, through comparison rather than direct explanation, we can
make our point. If we were to explain the joys or perils of memories
in a direct statement, it would likely be tedious; Emily Dickinson
spoke volumes in just one quatrain:

> The past is such a curious creature,
> To look her in the face
> A transport may reward us,
> Or a disgrace.

Curious, eh? Even though we know that the past is not a creature,
and has no face in which to look, the words somehow reach
us more than any direct statement, such as "Some memories are
pleasant, but others remind us of things of which we are ashamed."
Ugh. We would prefer Emily Dickinson's witty quatrain, any day.

To say that the past is a creature is really a **comparison**; the idea is that the past
is *similar to* a creature who, when you look her in the face, makes you feel
the transport of joy or the pain of disgrace over something you regret. Emily Dickinson
also wrote a different poem comparing nature to a mother; it is surely one
of the most beautiful, musical poems ever written about nature:

Nature, the gentlest mother,
Impatient of no child,
The feeblest or the waywardest,—
Her admonition mild

In forest and the hill
By traveller is heard,
Restraining rampant squirrel
Or too impetuous bird.

How fair her conversation,
A summer afternoon,—
Her household, her assembly;
And when the sun goes down

Her voice among the aisles
Incites the timid prayer
Of the minutest cricket
The most unworthy flower.

When all the children sleep
She turns as long away
As will suffice to light her lamps;
Then, bending from the sky,

With infinite affection
And infiniter care,
Her golden finger on her lip,
Wills silence everywhere.

the

minutest

cricket

106

The poem is so effective, we almost forget that *Nature* is an abstraction,
a concept we employ to group the world's processes and phenomena together.
Dickinson uses quatrains of **iambic trimeter**, with a few lines of **iambic tetrameter**
mixed in.

1   2   3
Her **ad** / mo **ni** / tion **mild**

1   2   3
A **sum** / mer **af** / ter **noon**

1   2   3
When **all** / the **chil** / dren **sleep**

1   2   3   4
As **will** / suf **fice** / to **light** / **her** lamps

Dickinson's talent was so great, the poem feels rhymed, even though

Which rhyme is most clever?

it really is not. The endings of lines one and three rarely resemble one another:
mother/waywardest; *hill/squirrel*; *conversation/assembly*; *aisles/cricket*; *sleep/lamps*;
affection/lip. Lines two and four sometimes rhyme, but sometimes are paired
in **near rhymes**: *child/mild*; *heard/bird*; *afternoon/down*; *prayer/flower*; *away/sky*; and
care/everywhere. There is more: look at the beautiful use of the consonant *r* in the second
quatrain; with a combination of **consonance** and **alliteration**, Dickinson gives the stanza
a rich sound:

> In forest and the hill
> By traveller is heard,
> Restraining rampant squirrel
> Or too impetuous bird.

Or look at the harmony of vowels and consonants in **unworthy flower**. Soft
sounds: *n*, *w*, *th*, *f*, *l*, *wo* and *ow*, *or* and *er*. Look at the *l*'s in the fifth quatrain: *all*, *children*,
sleep, *long*, *will*, *light*, *lamps*. Look at the *f*'s, *w*'s, *th*'s in the sixth quatrain. The gentlest
sounds, for the gentlest mother. It is absolute magic—a great poet at full power.

In Dickinson's poem about nature, we see how everything we have studied comes together. Dickinson has combined meter, rhyme, assonance, consonance, stanzas, and this creative comparison of the abstraction Nature to a person, a mother, with all of the things in nature as her children. The essence of the poem, that nature is positive rather than negative, is communicated first by comparing nature to a mother, and second by the use of poetic techniques to support that idea: gentle sounds for the gentle mother figure.

Even though we give great value to learning about the technical methods of poetry, it is still the ideas that come first. It is the ideas that drive the poem and guide what kinds of sounds, meters, and stanzas are appropriate. Ralph Waldo Emerson once wrote:

> For it is not metres, but a metre-making argument, that makes a poem,—a thought so passionate and alive, that, like the spirit of a plant or an animal, it has architecture of its own, and adorns nature with a new thing. The thought and the form are equal in the order of time, but in the order of genesis the thought is prior to the form.

Although it would be presumptuous to claim that we know, perfectly, how poets think, we must assume that Emerson is right. The thought is prior to the form. The poet first wants to say something about the world, and then works out the music for it.

When Dickinson wanted to reveal the inner characteristics of nature, and decided to compare nature to a mother, she was using a figure of speech called *personification*.

The thought is prior to the form.

FIGURES OF SPEECH

Figures of speech? Yes. Personification is a *figure of speech*. This means that it is not literally true: nature is not really a mother. The figure of the mother is not of the world, it is a *figure made of speech*.

Figures of speech are creations that help us communicate difficult things. Figures of speech can help to express things that are subtle or that are difficult to put into words directly. Poets have at their command an array of different figures of speech they can use to express ideas, and by combining the figures of speech with all of the other techniques of sound, meter, and stanza, they can help all humanity by expressing (at last!) things that all the rest of us have always wished we could say. In his masterpiece, "Song of Myself," the American poet Walt Whitman said,

> My words itch at your ears till you understand them.
> I do not say these things for a dollar
> or to fill up the time while I wait for a boat,
> (It is you talking just as much as myself, I act as the tongue of you,
> Tied in your mouth, in mine it begins to be loosen'd.)

A complete treatment of the figures of speech would require a long book. It takes pages just to list all of the figures of speech, but there are certain standard figures of speech that are best known and most widely used, including **metaphor, simile, personification, apostrophe, oxymoron, synecdoche,** and **metonymy.** Let's look at these in some detail.

FIGURES OF SPEECH—AN INTRODUCTORY SUMMARY

Figures of Speech are creative, indirect ways of expressing things; they usually involve comparisons that are not literally true.

Simile

A simile, pronounced SIM-ih-lee, is an openly expressed comparison using *like* or *as*; Robert Burns used simile in "My luve is like a red, red rose." An **epic simile** is an elaborate, highly developed simile; the model for this is the collection of extended similes that we find in Homer's *Iliad*.

Metaphor

A metaphor is an implied comparison. Shakespeare used metaphor in *Hamlet* to say that "Life is a walking shadow."

Synecdoche

A synecdoche, pronounced sin-ECK-do-kee, is a substitution of a part for the whole, as when Christopher Marlowe, in *Dr. Faustus*, wrote of Helen of Troy, "Was this the face that launched a thousand ships?" To call fifty ships fifty "sail" would be synecdoche. Synecdoche also works in reverse if we let the whole represent the part.

Metonymy

Metonymy is letting a related object represent something, such as "payment to the crown." To say that we "read Shakespeare" is metonymy; we actually read his plays and poems.

Personification

Personification is portraying an inanimate object, natural process, or animal as a person. Emily Dickinson portraying nature as a mother is personification.

Apostrophe

Apostrophe is addressing someone or something not present, as though present. Shelley's "Ode to the West Wind" is an example: "O wild, west wind..."

Oxymoron

An oxymoron is an expression that seems to contradict itself, but actually does not, such as "victory in defeat," or "bright darkness."

SIMILE and METAPHOR

A **simile** is a comparison that contains a word such as *like* or *as* to disclose
that it is a comparison. In a beautiful simile, Christina Rossetti wrote that "My heart is
like a singing bird." The easiest way to explain what a simile is, is to compare a simile to a
metaphor, which does not contain *like* or *as*. When Robert Burns said, "My love
is like a red, red rose," he was using a simile, but if he had said "My love *is* a red rose,"
that would have been a metaphor. A metaphor is like an equation. (That is a simile!) In
one of American poetry's most memorable metaphors, Emily Dickinson wrote, "Hope is
the thing with feathers, that perches in the soul." Similes and metaphors are
the two most common figures of speech.

My heart is a rolling ocean. (metaphor)
My heart is like a rolling ocean. (simile)

Alfred, Lord Tennyson, used similes in his long poem "In Memoriam A.H.H."
In two quatrains reflecting on the immense length of geologic time, and how
now there is land where once were oceans, and mountains rise and vanish in time,
Tennyson wrote:

There rolls the deep where grew the tree,	a
O earth, what changes hast thou seen!	b
There where the long street roars hath been	b
The stillness of the central sea.	a
The hills are shadows, and they flow	c
From form to form, and nothing stands;	d
They melt like mist, the solid lands,	d
Like clouds they shape themselves and go.	c

Do you see the similes? Hills melt *like mist*; solid lands *shape themselves like clouds*, and go.
Notice that Tennyson also used a metaphor in the second quatrain: the *hills are shadows*.

111

In one of the most powerful passages of British poetry, Byron described
the power and majesty of the sea, using a **simile** to compare a drowning to a drop
of rain. Here is the second stanza of "The Sea":

> Roll on, thou deep and dark blue Ocean,—roll!
> Ten thousand fleets sweep over thee in vain;
> Man marks the earth with ruin,—his control
> Stops with the shore;—upon the watery plain
> The wrecks are all thy deed, nor doth remain
> A shadow of man's ravage, save his own,
> When, for a moment, like a drop of rain,
> He sinks into thy depths with bubbling groan,
> Without a grave, unknelled, uncoffined, and unknown.

Wow. Notice the wave-like meter in the first line. Byron achieves the effect
by using spondees; he creates three stressed syllables in a row:

$$\underset{\text{spondee}}{\overset{1}{Roll\ on}} / \underset{\text{iamb}}{\overset{2}{thou\ deep}} / \underset{\text{iamb}}{\overset{3}{and\ dark}} / \underset{\text{spondee}}{\overset{4}{blue\ O}} / \underset{\text{iamb}}{\overset{5}{cean,—roll!}}$$

As for the image of drowning, Byron was not being gruesome;
this happens. The roaring sea has claimed the lives of untold sailors and sea passengers.
Its power is legendary. Byron's simile comparing the sinking of a person
from the surface to nothing more permanent than a drop of rain communicates, more
than any direct statement could, the overwhelming force of the sea.

What we are seeing here is one example of how powerful a figure of speech
can be.

Like a drop of rain, **he sinks into thy depths.**

William Wordsworth used a simile in the first stanza of his poem "Daffodils," to compare loneliness to a solitary cloud, moving above the valley:

I wandered lonely as a cloud	a
That floats on high o'er vales and hills,	b
When all at once I saw a crowd,	a
A host, of golden daffodils;	b
Beside the lake, beneath the trees,	c
Fluttering and dancing in the breeze.	c

Wordsworth wrote this sestet in iambic tetrameter. There are four sestets in the poem.

In "To a Skylark" Percy Shelley used a brilliant simile to describe the soaring bird:

Higher still and higher
From the earth thou springest,
Like a cloud of fire;
The blue deep thou wingest,
And singing still dost soar, and soaring ever singest.

What did Shelley mean, comparing the skylark to a cloud of fire?

Why might a poet use a metaphor instead of a simile?

METAPHOR
We could say, if we dared to, that a metaphor is an implied simile. In other words, if I say that the future is a turned-off television, everyone knows that I don't really think that. What I mean, what I am implying, is that the future is like a turned-off television. So a metaphor is really an implied simile. I mean that A is *like* B, but I say A *is* B, and let it be understood. In a famous metaphor, John Donne wrote that no man is an island, that we are all connected: "Every man is a part of the continent." A metaphor gives the reader credit for being intelligent!

In Shakespeare's *Romeo and Juliet*, Romeo has sneaked into Juliet's family compound, and is hiding in the bushes, looking up at her window and wishing she would appear. Then, to his wondering eyes, she appears! First, he sees a light at the window; he whispers:

> But soft! What light through yonder window breaks?
> It is the east, and Juliet is the sun!

Romeo's metaphor is that *Juliet is the sun*. Of course, she is not. The equation of Juliet=sun is an implied comparison, expressing the light that Juliet brings to his heart.

In "Leaves of Grass," Walt Whitman used a brilliant metaphor to explain the miracle of life:

> A child said What is the grass? fetching it to me with full hands.
> How could I answer the child? I do not know what it is any
>   more than he.
> I guess it must be the flag of my disposition, out of hopeful
>   green stuff woven.

The grass is the hopeful, green flag of my disposition; this is one of the greatest metaphors in American literature. Whitman is a hero to poets around the world.

In 1867 after the American Civil War had brought industrial-strength killing to the madness of war, Matthew Arnold (1822-1888) wrote a moving poem, very modern in its tone and style, giving early expression to the modern sensibility of human isolation in an age of lost faith. Arnold beautifully compared the erosion of faith in society to the receding of the sea. "Dover Beach" is a poem of five stanzas, and Arnold used the withdrawal of the sea/faith as the guiding **metaphor** of the poem. If you look closely, you will also see two **similes** in the final stanza.

Quite aside from the technical details of the poem, the metaphor of the sea is exceptional. It has a panoramic vista to it that shocks us with a vivid sense of the widespread change in society. The final plea, "Let us be true to one another," is very moving.

Dover Beach
Matthew Arnold

The sea is calm tonight,
The tide is full, the moon lies fair
Upon the straits; on the French coast the light
Gleams and is gone; the cliffs of England stand,
Glimmering and vast, out in the tranquil bay.
Come to the window, sweet is the night air!

Only, from the long line of spray
Where the sea meets the moon-blanched land,
Listen! you hear the grating roar
Of pebbles which the waves draw back, and fling,
At their return, up the high strand,
Begin, and cease, and then again begin,
With tremulous cadence slow, and bring
The eternal note of sadness in.

Sophocles long ago
Heard it on the Agean, and it brought
Into his mind the turbid ebb and flow
Of human misery; we
Find also in the sound a thought,
Hearing it by this distant northern sea.

The Sea of Faith
Was once, too, at the full, and round earth's shore
Lay like the folds of a bright girdle furled.
But now I only hear
Its melancholy, long, withdrawing roar,
Retreating, to the breath
Of the night wind, down the vast edges drear
And naked shingles of the world.

Ah, love, let us be true
To one another! for the world, which seems
To lie before us like a land of dreams,
So various, so beautiful, so new,
Hath really neither joy, nor love, nor light,
Nor certitude, nor peace, nor help for pain;
And we are here as on a darkling* plain
Swept with confused alarms of struggle and flight,
Where ignorant armies clash by night.

And we are here as on a darkling plain
Swept with confused alarms of struggle and flight,
Where ignorant armies clash by night.

*Darkling means in the dark or growing dark.

DEPTH OF COMPARISON—A POINT OF DISCUSSION

It is extraordinary how profound (deep) metaphors and
similes can be. At times, they seem to take us into zones of recognition that ordinary
words cannot enter, and when we try to explain the comparison, words fail us.
One striking example of this comes from William Butler Yeats, who
knew a beautiful woman, Maud Gonne; she was a political revolutionary,
fierce in her dedication to Irish independence, and she did not return Yeats's feelings.
In his poem "No Second Troy," Yeats compared her to Helen of Troy,
whose beauty caused the destruction of an entire civilization:

Maud Gonne

Why should I blame her that she filled my days
With misery, or that she would of late
Have taught to ignorant men most violent ways,
Or hurled the little streets upon the great,
Had they but courage equal to desire?
What could have made her peaceful with a mind
That nobleness made simple as a fire,
With beauty like a tightened bow, a kind
That is not natural in an age like this,
Being high and solitary and most stern?
Why, what could she have done, being what she is?
Was there another Troy for her to burn?

The question is, what do you think Yeats meant in his simile that Maud Gonne's beauty
was "like a tightened bow"? This is not the sort of question that necessarily has a right
answer; it is an interpretive question. What would be the difference between beauty that
was like a tightened bow, and beauty that was not?

With beauty like a tightened bow...

SYNECDOCHE and METONYMY

Just as simile and metaphor are related ideas, synecdoche and metonymy are related ideas. **Synecdoche** (sin-ECK-do-kee) is letting a part of something represent the whole, as when we say, "All hands on deck." We do not imagine that a bunch of hands will come jumping out of the ship's hold and go skittering across the briny deck on their fingers. We only use the term *hands* because hands symbolize all of the work that must be done—by hand. Oddly, letting the whole represent the part is also considered synecdoche. **Metonymy** (meh-TAH-no-me) is similar, but instead of letting a part of something represent it, we use a related object to represent it, as when we say that the subjects pay taxes to the *crown*. Again, we do not imagine that people are going up to a crown and tossing in money; we are only using the crown as a symbol of the state.

synecdoche a part

metonymy related object

Having said these things, we must now go back to Yeats's poem and look at the fourth line, where he says that Maud Gonne would recently have taught ignorant men most violent ways and "hurled the little streets upon the great." Clearly, Yeats did not mean that Maud Gonne would be heaving streets around, like a human bulldozer; rather, it is a case of **metonymy**. Maud Gonne wanted the poor, exploited (little) Irish people to rise in rebellion against (great) Great Britain. By using the images of poor and wealthy streets to convey an image of people's lives, Yeats captures the idea vividly.

hurled the little streets upon the great

PERSONIFICATION

We have seen personification already in Emily Dickinson's comparison
of nature to a mother. Personification is depicting something as a person,
giving it human qualities. A lovely example of personification comes
from Percy Shelley's poem "To the Moon," which also has a simile. Here
is the complete poem:

Art thou pale for weariness	a
Of climbing heaven and gazing on the earth,	b
Wandering companionless	a
Among the stars that have a different birth,—	b
And ever changing, like a joyless eye	c
That finds no object worth its constancy?	c

Did you notice that the sestet rhyme scheme, ababcc, is the same one Wordsworth
used in his poem about the daffodils (I wandered lonely as a cloud...)? In this poem
Shelley **personified** the moon and addressed it; we cannot help thinking that
Shelley identified with the moon, and that he was really talking about (and to)
himself.

APOSTROPHE

Shelley not only personified the moon, he used an **apostrophe**, because
he addressed (spoke to) the moon. An apostrophe is when a poet
directly addresses something not real or not really there; the moon-person
Shelley was addressing was only an abstraction, a figure of speech, not of nature,
and so this was an apostrophe.

Art thou pale for weariness...

One of the most delightful examples of **personification** is this
poem by G.K. Chesterton, in which he personifies many things, all doing
things they normally can not do! It contains five stanzas, quatrains, is called "A Certain
Evening":

That night the whole world mingled,
The souls were babes at play,
And angel danced with devil,
And God cried, "Holiday!"

The sea had climbed the mountain peaks,
And shouted to the stars
To come to play: and down they came
Splashing in happy wars.

The pine grew apples for a whim,
The cart-horse built a nest;
The oxen flew, the flowers sang,
The sun rose in the west.

Which line
is the most
creative and
original?

And 'neath the load of many worlds,
The lowest life God made
Lifted his huge and heavy limbs
And into heaven strayed,

To where the highest life God made
Before his presence stands:
But God Himself cried, "Holiday!"
And she gave me both her hands.

Something to think about: are these quatrains **ballad** stanzas? Why or why not?

OXYMORON

An oxymoron is a combination of words, usually an adjective
and noun, that seems contradictory; notable examples are "jumbo shrimp"
and Shakespeare's "sweet sorrow" from *Romeo and Juliet*. The political
commentator George Will has said that the term "domestic cat" is
an oxymoron! Among the great poetry containing oxymorons
is this passage, spoken by Theseus who is reading a message written by a fool, in V. i.
(that means Act V, scene 1) of Shakespeare's play *A Midsummer Night's Dream*.
The fool proposes to perform a play, but writes a bizarre description,
misusing words, such as *tedious* and *mirth*, because he does not really know what
they mean! The noble Theseus reads the first two lines, then comments in
the second three:

"A tedious brief scene of young Pyramus
And his love Thisby; very tragical mirth."
Merry and tragical! tedious and brief!
That is hot ice and wondrous strange snow.
How shall we find the concord of this discord?

Of course, in order to be tedious (tiresome), something must be long,
and can not be brief; to be tragical, something must be sad, and cannot
be mirth. Theseus describes the passage, appropriately, as *hot ice*!

Oxymorons, very often, make us laugh! They were an important part
of Shakespeare's funniest scenes.

A FIGURE OF SPEECH LAB

We have studied seven figures of speech, including **simile**, **metaphor**, **synecdoche**, **metonymy**, **personification**, **apostrophe**, and **oxymoron**. Let's have some fun; let's write a poem, in one of the stanza forms we have learned. The goal is to use as many of the seven figures of speech as possible, and even more than once if possible. Since the theme of this book is our common humanity, you might want to write your poem in conjunction with a photograph of a person, as we have done before.

Sonnet for That Bat, Arman
Michael Clay Thompson

Arman was now a pendulum, a swing,
Suspending upside down, the grassy sky
Above him soaring o'er the bluey scene
That gaped below the arc his feet described.
He dangled, hangled, like a bat, and squeaked,
"O Gravity," he cackled, "let me make
Another swing before I fall, and strike
The grass above my head; I got no brake!"
He chuckled like hyenas, face full red,
A ripe tomato. Soon these gruffy mugs
Would drop him, ugh, and up he'd fall, his head
Colliding with the lawn, green ceiling rug.
The cruel stick had had enough, it dropped
The hapless bat, Arman, hands flapping—stopped.

A FIGURE OF SPEECH LAB

We have studied seven figures of speech, including **simile**, **metaphor**, **synecdoche**, **metonymy**, **personification**, **apostrophe**, and **oxymoron**. Identify each of the following twenty-five figures of speech. Then find a photograph of people doing something fun, and write an example of each figure of speech to accompany the photo.

1.   The flock of gulls had a diverse unity.
2.   "O Seagull, give me a break," I said.
3.   The rolling ocean was like a blue golf course.
4.   The boys were seagulls, too.
5.   The seagulls laughed at the boys.
6.   The gulls were like a cluster of winged grapes.
7.   "Hello Sky," he said.
8.   The sandy strand was a blue kaliedoscope.
9.   The flock of wings arose into the sunset.
10. The cries flew over our heads to the west.
11. The gull gaped with a silent squawk.
12. He flapped his arms like a seagull.
13. He ran after the birds, as a dog chases a rabbit.
14. The ocean watched the boys and chuckled wavily.
15. The orange sky sank slowly below the horizon.
16. The beaks swooped low to snatch fish.
17. The birds communicated in silent conversation.
18. The gulls rose into the air like drops of a fountain.
19. The horizon was a string of black yarn.
20. Our feet raced down the sand.
21. The sails turned back toward the harbor.
22. The dull flash of minnows lit the water.
23. The waves chuckled in watery agreement.
24. "Stay here, Sun," we cried.
25. The polkadots flew left.

Let's combine all of our thinking processes and examine one poem, to see
what we can notice. Look for meter, stanza, sound, and figures of speech. We will
examine a poem by James Leigh Hunt (1784-1859). Inspect the poem with great
care, and when you have found everything you can, turn the page to see our analysis.
A note: Sesostris was Rameses II, king of Egypt cerca 1300 B.C.; today, his badly
constructed pyramid is crumbling into sand. The "southern beam" is a reference
to Cleopatra. Hunt is believed to have written this poem in competition with
Keats and Shelley.

The Nile
James Leigh Hunt

It flows through old hushed Egypt and its sands,
Like some grave mighty thought threading a dream,
And times and things, as in that vision, seem
Keeping along it their eternal stands,—
Caves, pillars, pyramids, the shepherd bands
That roamed through the young world, the glory extreme
Of high Sesostris, and that southern beam,
The laughing queen that caught the world's great hands.
Then comes a mightier silence, stern and strong,
As of a world left empty of its throng,
And the void weighs on us; and then we wake,
And hear the fruitful stream lapsing along
Twixt villages, and think how we shall take
Our own calm journey on for human sake.

Observations

1. The poem is sonnet, a variation of the English sonnet. Charles Algernon Swinburne used this same rhyme scheme, abbaabbaccdcdd, in a sequence of sonnets on the death of Robert Browning.

2. A brilliant primary simile: the Nile flows through Egypt like a thought threading a dream.

3. Notice the assonance on the *e* in the first quatrain: *Egypt, dream, seem, keeping, eternal*.

4. Look at the variations of *o* sound in line six: *roamed, through, young, world, glory*.

5. Do you see the internal rhyme of *thought* and *caught*? Notice that the two words land in exactly the same metrical position in their lines. Hunt separated them so they would not be noticed, but would still play their echo in the back of our minds.

> Line 2: Like some / grave migh / ty **thought** / threading / a dream,
> Line 8: The laugh / ing queen / that **caught** / the world's great hands.

6. Notice the consonance on the *s* sound in line nine: the word *silence* has a *c* in it, but the sound of that *c* is an *s* sound that goes with the alliterated *s*'s in the rest of the line.

7. The words *weigh* and *wake* in line eleven are **reverse rhyme**; they rhyme in their first syllables, not in their last! In that line, notice the alliteration of *weigh*, *we*, and *wake*.

8. In line six, notice the **amphisbaenic** sounds of:

roamed, th**r**ough, w**o**rld, and g**lo**ry

9. In line thirteen notice the consonance on the *k* sound in *twixt*, *think*, and *take*.

10. Notice the **caesura** in line eleven. And the void weighs on us // and then we wake.

11. Notice the play of sound in:

pillars, shepherd, eternal, world, and southern.

12. Notice the **apophany**-like structure in line six of: That **roamed**...ex**treme**.

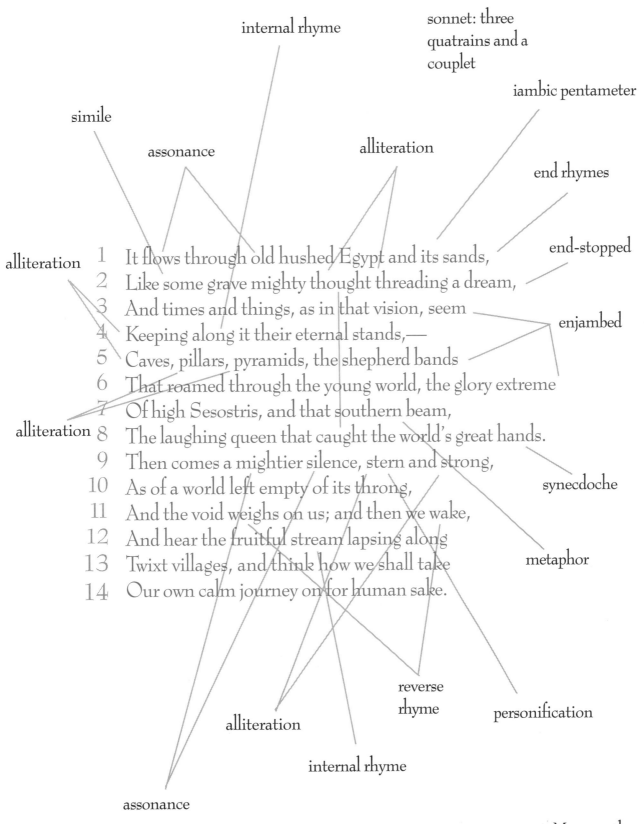

internal rhyme

sonnet: three
quatrains and a
couplet

iambic pentameter

simile

assonance

alliteration

end rhymes

end-stopped

alliteration

1 It flows through old hushed Egypt and its sands,
2 Like some grave mighty thought threading a dream,
3 And times and things, as in that vision, seem
4 Keeping along it their eternal stands,—
5 Caves, pillars, pyramids, the shepherd bands
6 That roamed through the young world, the glory extreme
7 Of high Sesostris, and that southern beam,
8 The laughing queen that caught the world's great hands.
9 Then comes a mightier silence, stern and strong,
10 As of a world left empty of its throng,
11 And the void weighs on us; and then we wake,
12 And hear the fruitful stream lapsing along
13 Twixt villages, and think how we shall take
14 Our own calm journey on for human sake.

enjambed

synecdoche

alliteration

metaphor

reverse
rhyme

personification

alliteration

internal rhyme

assonance

More on the
next page...

It is interesting to note that the entire poem contains only two sentences:

> It flows through old hushed Egypt and its sands,
> Like some grave mighty thought threading a dream,
> And times and things, as in that vision, seem
> Keeping along it their eternal stands,—
> Caves, pillars, pyramids, the shepherd bands
> That roamed through the young world, the glory extreme
> Of high Sesostris, and that southern beam,
> The laughing queen that caught the world's great hands.
>
> Then comes a mightier silence, stern and strong,
> As of a world left empty of its throng,
> And the void weighs on us; and then we wake,
> And hear the fruitful stream lapsing along
> Twixt villages, and think how we shall take
> Our own calm journey on for human sake.

Q Which stanza do you like more?

This observation is immensely beneficial in understanding the ideas of the poem. We have, essentially two ideas—two ideas that combine to make the great Nile River and its deeper realities real to us. First, the river flows, like a thought threading a dream, through the extraordinary, still-reverberating, remnants of its past. Second, the river moves into the great, cosmic silence of the desert, and the void weighs on us, putting us to sleep. In the final couplet, we see that this river is a great metaphor for ourselves, that we move through our own life, as though threading a dream, and that we move through our own memories of our own past, and will continue to move forward into the human experiences that await us.

If we look at a few details of grammar in the poem, we find good things:

It	flows	through	old	hushed	Egypt	and	its	sands.

I.   pron.   v.   prep.   adj.   adj.   n.   conj.   pron.   n.

II.   subject   predicate

III.   --------------------prepositional phrase--------------------

IV.   ----------------------------one independent clause------------------------

Comment: The introductory sentence of the sonnet begins in the clearest way. The subject/predicate set *it/flows* gives us the immediate sense of the Nile moving, and the rest of the clause is an extended prepositional phrase with a compound object of preposition. The river flows through 1) Egypt and 2) its sands. But the proper noun *Egypt* is modified by two adjectives: *old* and *hushed*.

Then	comes	a	mightier	silence,	stern	and	strong.

I.   adv.   v.   adj.   adj.   n.   adj.   conj.   adj.

II.   predicate   subject

III.   -------no prepositional, appositive, or verbal phrase---------

IV.   ------------------------------one independent clause-------------------------

Comment: The first words of the second sentence are even more interesting because they contain an instance of **hyperbaton** (hi-PURR-baton), which is a disruption of normal word order; in this case, the verb-predicate *comes* precedes the noun-subject *silence*, which is surrounded by a cloud of four adjectives, two on either side. By putting the subject last, Hunt was able to give great presence to the silence of the desert, to push it forward as the dominant experience of the sentence. After the subject, we have a beautiful compound adjective *stern and strong*.

CONCLUDING THOUGHTS

It may seem that we have gone into incredible depth in our look
at poetry, and yet, just as we have only really glanced at the universal
characteristics that unite us all as human beings, we have also only really
glanced at poetry. There is much, much more to learn in terms of technique,
and there is a vast array of astounding poems to experience which we have
only glimpsed in our study.

When we reflect on everything that we have learned, what are we
to make of it? What does it all mean?

We could say that the two themes of the book, the nature of poetry
and the nature of humanity, are essentially one, for poets are part
of humanity, and their artistic work as poets is an example of humanity's
most extreme efforts to understand ourselves and our world, and to express
the conclusions through language, language that is pushed to its maximum limits.

One of the things that connects all of us in the world, one of the most important
things that connects us, is language. All cultures in the world have language.
There are thousands of different languages on our planet, and some of them
are extremely different from English, and yet it is almost shocking when,
for example, we are watching a documentary film about a remote tribe of people
somewhere in a wilderness, and the language sounds like nothing we have ever
heard, but then when the strange conversation is translated, it could have been said by
our neighbor next door. We are all just people. We are kids, and teenagers,
and grownups. We are old and young, happy and sad, laughing and quiet.
We all use langauge; we talk to our family, to our friends, to ourselves.

What poets do is to become extreme artists in this one extremely human
thing, language. A great poem may seem effortless, but when we look closely at the art
involved, we can see that it was not. In a way, poets are like other extreme artists,
such as composers or symphonies or sculptors—poets often devote almost unimaginable
hours and talent and intensity to the perfect expression of an idea that people
will consider important.

What we have done in this book is to take a close-up look
at some of the ways they do that.

My Heart Leaps Up
William Wordsworth, 1802

My heart leaps up when I behold
A rainbow in the sky.
So was it when my life began;
So is it now I am a man;
So be it when I grow old,
Or let me die!
The Child is father of the Man;
And I could wish my days to be
Bound each to each by natural piety.

How is the child the father of the man?

STUDY POEMS

On these pages, there are poems that you can think about,
and continue reflection about what poetry is, how it works, and what it has
to do with our lives. Study is a *very* good thing. To study is to think.
It is one of our greatest and most beautiful human powers. We are the only living
organism that can study! By studying, we realize.

Cataract On Mount Lu

Li Bo, translated by Xu Yuan Zhong

The sunlit Censer peak exhales a wreath of cloud;
Like an upended stream the cataract sounds loud.
Its torrent dashes down three thousand feet from high,
As if the Silver River fell from azure sky.

Censer: a vessel for perfumes; esp. one in which incense is burned.
Silver River: the Chinese name for the Milky Way.

This is the land the sunset washes,
These are the Banks of the Yellow Sea;
Where it rose, or whither it rushes,
These are the western mystery!

Night after night her purple traffic
Strews the landing with opal bales;
Merchantmen poise upon horizons,
Dip, and vanish like orioles!

- Emily Dickinson

Adam's Curse
William Butler Yeats

We sat together at one summer's end,
That beautiful mild woman, your close friend,
And you and I, and talked of poetry.
I said, "A line will take us hours maybe;
Yet if it does not seem a moment's thought,
Our stitching and unstitching has been naught.
Better go down upon your marrow-bones
And scrub a kitchen pavement, or break stones
Like an old pauper, in all kinds of weather;
For to articulate sweet sounds together
Is to work harder than all these, and yet
Be thought an idler by the noisy set
Of bankers, schoolmasters, and clergymen
The martyrs call the world."

Some Elements of Poetry

SOUND: the manipulation of language sounds.
Rhyme: identical sounds at the endings of words, as *rule* and *fool*.
End rhyme: rhyme at the ends of lines of poetry.
Internal Rhyme: rhymes inside the lines, or a word inside a line that rhymes with a word at the end of a line.
Eye-rhyme: also called *sight rhyme*, eye-rhymes are rhymes that look alike, but do not sound alike; they rhyme to the eye, not to the ear, such as *through* and *enough*.
Rhyme scheme: using letters to show the arrangement of rhyme, such as ababcdcdefefgg for a sonnet.
Masculine rhyme: one-syllable rhyme, as *road* and *strode*.
Feminine rhyme: two-syllable rhyme, as *fiddle* and *griddle*.
Onomatopoeia: a word that sounds like what it describes: *boom*!
Alliteration: the repetition of initial vowels or consonants, such as *slurp* and *soul*, or *omit* and *open*.
Assonance: the repetition of vowel sounds: *make* and *flame*.
Consonance: the repetition of consonant sounds: *edit* and *mode*.
Stopped consonants: consonants that stop the breath: PB TD KG.
Reversal: a rearrangement of repeated sounds, as *wall* and *law*.
End-stopped: a pause (period or comma) at the end of the line.
Enjambed: no pause at the end of the line.
Near rhyme: also called *slant rhyme*, near rhyme is almost rhyme, as *reward* and *rearward*.
Half-double Rhyme: the last syllable of one word rhymes with the next-to-last syllable of another! The words *man* and *savanna* are examples.
Elided Rhyme: there are two syllables that would be a perfect rhyme except for the vowel in the second syllable. The words *livid* and *lived* are an elided rhyme.
Amphisbaenic Rhyme: two syllables are identical, but in reverse! Examples would be *stick* and *kits*, *kill* and *lick*, or (almost) *Nile* and *lion*.
Reverse Rhyme: When words share the first syllable sound, such as *native*, *nature*, *nadir*, and *nation*.
Half Rhyme or Apophany: when two syllables share their beginning and ending consonants, but not the vowel in between. The words *stand* and *stunned* are apophany, as are *cattle* and *kettle*.

METER: the pattern of rhythm of syllables.
Stress: the emphasis given to certain syllables in words.
Foot: the repeating unit of meter.
Iamb: a two-syllable foot with the stress on the second syllable. The English language is

naturally iambic, and Shakespeare used iambs for the speeches of good or noble figures.

Trochee: a two-syllable foot with the stress on the first syllable. Trochees are anti-iambic, and are often used to convey a feeling of danger or evil. Shakespeare used trochaic tetrameter for the witches' chant in *Macbeth*: Double, double, toil and trouble.

Anapest: a three-syllable foot with the stress on the third.

Dactyl: a three-syllable foot with the stress on the first.

Spondee: a two-syllable foot with both syllables stressed.

Catalexis: dropping an unstressed syllable from the end of a trochaic or dactylic line.

Pyrrhic foot: a two-syllable foot, both syllables unstressed.

Amphibrach: rare; a three syllable foot, with the middle syllable stressed: *petunia*.

Amphimacer: rare: a three-syllable foot, the middle syllable is short, and the first and third are long:

Caesura: a natural break or pause in a line of poetry, usually near the middle of the line, usually marked by punctuation. We indicate a caesura with a double slash //.

Iambic pentameter: five iambs to a line of ten syllables. Sonnets, rime royal, and heroic couplets all use iambic pentameter.

Trimeter: a three-foot line.

Tetrameter: a four-foot line.

Pentameter: a five-foot line.

Hexameter: a six-foot line.

Heptameter: a seven-foot line

Octameter: an eight-foot line

STANZA: a part of a poem, based on form of meter and rhyme.

Couplet: a two-line stanza

Triplet: a three-line stanza, also called a *tercet*

Quatrain: a four-line stanza

Quintet: a five-line stanza, also called a *quinquain*

Sestet: a six-line stanza

Septet: a seven-line stanza

Octet: an eight-line stanza

Ballad: a quatrain alternating iambic tetrameter in lines one and three with iambic trimeter in lines two and four. The rhyme scheme of a ballad is abcb.

Limerick: a five-line nonsense poem, mostly in anapest, rhyme scheme aabba. Lines one, two, and five have three feet, but lines three and four have only two feet.

English/Shakespearean Sonnet: a fourteen-line poem of four stanzas, three quatrains and a couplet. The rhyme scheme is abab cdcd efef gg.

Italian/Petrarchan Sonnet: a fourteen-line poem of an octave and a sestet. abba abba cde cde.

Spenserian Sonnet: a variation of the English sonnet that Edmund Spenser developed; it interlocks the sonnet's three quatrains' rhymes, abab bcbc cdcd ee, rather than moving to new rhymes in each quatrain. The Spenserian sonnet has not been widely used, but it shows us that within the sonnet form there are interesting variations possible.

Submerged Sonnet: a sonnet that is concealed within a longer work.

Rime Royal: seven lines of iambic pentameter, rhyme scheme ababbcc.

Heroic couplets: rhymed couplets of iambic pentameter.

Terza rima: a special form of **triplet**. Terza rima is a three-line stanza, usually iambic pentameter, in which the first and third lines of each stanza rhyme, and the middle line becomes the beginning rhyme of the next stanza. The most famous poem written in terza rima is Percy Shelley's "Ode to the West Wind."

Villanelle: a poem of nineteen lines: five tercets and a quatrain. There are only two rhymes in a villanelle! All of the tercets rhyme aba, and the quatrain rhymes abaa, so the poem is aba aba aba aba aba abaa. To make it more complicated, lines 6, 12, and 18 repeat line 1, and lines 9, 15, and 19 repeat line 3! There is no specified meter for a villanelle.

FIGURES OF SPEECH: Special poetic ways of expressing things, especially comparisons that are not literally true.

Simile: an openly expressed comparison using *like* or *as*; Robert Burns used simile in "My luve is like a red, red rose."

Epic simile: an elaborate, highly developed simile; the model for this is the very long, wonderful similes that we find in Homer's *Iliad*.

Metaphor: an implied comparison. Shakespeare used metaphor in *Hamlet* to say that "Life is a walking shadow."

Personification: portraying an object as a person.

Apostrophe: addressing someone or something not present, as though present. Shelley's "Ode to the West Wind" is an example: "O wild, west wind..."

Oxymoron: an expression that seems to contradict itself, but actually does not, such as "victory in defeat," or "bright darkness."

Synecdoche: pronounced sin-ECK-do-kee, a substitution of a part for the whole, as when Christopher Marlowe, in *Dr. Faustus*, wrote of Helen of Troy, "Was this the face that launched a thousand ships?" To call fifty ships fifty "sail" would be synecdoche. Synecdoche also works in reverse if we let the whole represent the part.

Metonymy: letting a related object represent something, such as "payment to the crown." To say we "read Shakespeare" is metonymy; we actually read his plays and poems.